Born to Smoke

NICOTINE AND GENETICS

Tobacco: The Deadly Drug

Born to Smoke: Nicotine and Genetics

Burning Money: The Cost of Smoking

But All My Friends Smoke:
Cigarettes and Peer Pressure

But Smoking Makes Me Happy: The Link Between
Nicotine and Depression

Cash Crop to Cash Cow:
The History of Tobacco and Smoking in America

False Images, Deadly Promises:
Smoking and the Media

No More Butts: Kicking the Tobacco Habit

Putting Out the Fire: Smoking and the Law

Smokeless Tobacco: Not a Safe Alternative

Teenagers and Tobacco:
Nicotine and the Adolescent Brain

Thousands of Deadly Chemicals:
Smoking and Health

Born to Smoke

Nicotine and Genetics

by
David Hunter

Born to Smoke: Nicotine and Genetics

MASON CREST PUBLISHERS INC.
370 Reed Road
Broomall, Pennsylvania 19008
(866)MCP-BOOK (toll free)
www.masoncrest.com

First Printing

9 8 7 6 5 4 3 2 1

ISBN: 978-1-4222-0243-2
ISBN (series) 978-1-4222-0230-2
        Library of Congress Cataloging-in-Publication Data

Hunter, David
    Born to smoke : nicotine and genetics / David Hunter.
      p. cm. — (Tobacco: the deadly drug)
  Includes bibliographical references and index.
  ISBN 978-1-4222-0243-2   ISBN 978-1-4222-1325-4
  1. Nicotine addiction—Genetic aspects—Juvenile literature. I. Title.
  RC567.H86 2009
  616.86′5042—dc22
                            2008013218

Design by MK Bassett-Harvey.
Produced by Harding House Publishing Service, Inc.
www.hardinghousepages.com
Cover design by Peter Culotta.
Printed in The United States of America.

Contents

Introduction *6*

1 The Dangers of Smoking *11*

2 Understanding Nicotine Addiction *21*

3 The Basics of Genetics *33*

4 A Genetic Connection *51*

5 Body Chemistry *67*

6 Overcoming Nicotine Addiction *85*

Further Reading *104*

For More Information *105*

Bibliography *106*

Index *108*

Picture Credits *111*

Author/Consultant Biographies *112*

Introduction

Tobacco has been around for centuries. In fact, it played a major role in the early history of the United States. Tobacco use has fallen into and out of popularity, sometimes based on gender roles or class, or more recently, because of its effects on health. The books in the Mason Crest series Tobacco: The Deadly Drug, provide readers with a look at many aspects of tobacco use. Most important, the series takes a serious look at why smoking is such a hard habit to break, even with all of the available information about its harmful effects.

The primary ingredient in tobacco products that keeps people coming back for another cigarette is nicotine. Nicotine is a naturally occurring chemical in the tobacco plant. As plants evolved over millions of years, they developed the ability to produce chemical defenses against being eaten by animals. Nicotine is the tobacco plant's chemical defense weapon. Just as too much nicotine can make a person feel dizzy and nauseated, so the same thing happens to animals that might otherwise eat unlimited quantities of the tobacco plant.

Nicotine, in small doses, produces mildly pleasurable (rewarding) experiences, leading many people to dose themselves repeatedly throughout the day. People carefully dose themselves with nicotine to maximize the rewarding experience. These periodic hits of tobacco also help people avoid unpleasant (toxic) effects, such as dizziness, nausea, trembling, and sweating, which can occur when someone takes in an excessive amount of nicotine. These unpleasant effects are sometimes seen when a person smokes for the first time.

Although nicotine is the rewarding component of cigarettes, it is not the cause of many diseases that trouble smokers, such as lung cancer, heart attacks, and strokes. Many of the thousands of other chemicals in the cigarette are responsible for the increased risk for these diseases among smokers. In some cases, medical research has identified cancer-causing chemicals in the burning cigarette. More research is needed, because our understanding of exactly how cigarette smoking causes many forms of cancer, lung diseases (emphysema, bronchitis), heart attacks, and strokes is limited, as is our knowledge on the effects of secondhand smoke.

The problem with smoking also involves addiction. But what is addiction? Addiction refers to a pattern of behavior, lasting months to years, in which a person engages in the intense, daily use of a pleasure-producing (rewarding) activity, such as smoking. This type of use has medically and personally negative effects for the person. As an example of negative medical consequences, consider that heavy smoking (nicotine addiction) leads to heart attacks and lung cancer. As an example of negative personal consequences, consider that heavy smoking may cause a loss of friendship, because the friend can't tolerate the smoke and/or the odor.

Nicotine addiction includes tolerance and withdrawal. New smokers typically start with fewer than five cigarettes per day. Gradually, as the body becomes adapted to the presence of nicotine, greater amounts are required to obtain the same rewarding effects, and the person eventually smokes fifteen to twenty or more cigarettes per day. This is tolerance, meaning that more drug is needed to achieve the same rewarding effects. The brain becomes "wired" differently after long-term exposure to nicotine, allowing the brain to tolerate levels of nicotine that would otherwise be toxic and cause nausea, vomiting, dizziness and anxiety.

When a heavy smoker abruptly stops smoking, irritability, headache, sleeplessness, anxiety, and difficulty concentrating all develop within half a day and trouble the smoker for one to two weeks. These withdrawal effects are generally the opposite of those produced by the drug. They are another external sign that the brain has become wired differently because of long-term exposure to nicotine. The withdrawal effects described above are accompanied by craving. For the nicotine addict, craving is a state of mind in which having a cigarette seems the most important thing in life at the moment. For the nicotine addict, craving is a powerful urge to smoke.

Nicotine addiction, then, can be understood as heavy, daily use over months to years (with tolerance and withdrawal), despite negative consequences. Now that we have definitions of *nicotine* and *addiction*, why read the books in this series? The answer is simple: tobacco is available everywhere to persons of all ages. The books in the series TOBACCO: THE DEADLY DRUG are about understanding the beginnings, natural history, and consequences of nicotine addiction. If a teenager smokes at least one cigarette daily for a month, that person has an 80 percent chance of becoming a lifetime, nicotine-addicted, daily smoker, with all the negative consequences.

But the series is not limited to those topics. What are the characteristic beginnings of nicotine addiction? Nicotine addiction typically begins between the ages of twelve and twenty, when most young people decide to try a first cigarette. Because cigarettes are available everywhere in our society, with little restriction on purchase, nearly everyone is faced with the decision to take a puff from that first cigarette. Whether this first puff leads to a lifetime of nicotine addiction depends on several factors. Perhaps the most important factor is DNA (genetics), as twin studies tell us that most of the risk for nicotine addiction is genetic, but there is a large role for nongenetic factors (environment), such as the smoking habits of friends. Research is needed to identify the specific genetic and environmental factors that shape a person's decision to continue to smoke after that first cigarette. Books in the series also address how peer pressure and biology affect one's likelihood of smoking and possibly becoming addicted.

It is difficult to underestimate the power of nicotine addiction. It causes smokers to continue to smoke despite life-threatening events. When heavy smokers have a heart attack, a life-threatening event often directly related to smoking, they spend a week or more in the hospital where they cannot smoke. So they are discharged after enforced abstinence. Even though they realize that smoking contributed strongly to the heart attack, half of them return to their former smoking habits within three weeks of leaving the hospital. This decision to return to smoking increases the risk of a second heart attack. Nicotine addiction can influence powerfully the choices we make, often prompting us to make choices that put us at risk.

TOBACCO: THE DEADLY DRUG doesn't stop with the whys and the hows of smoking and addiction. The series includes books that provide readers with tools they can use to not take that first cigarette, how they can stand up to negative peer pressure, and know when they are being unfairly influenced by the media. And if they do become smokers, books in the series provide information about how they can stop.

If nicotine addiction can be a powerful negative effect, then giving people information that might help them decide to avoid—or stop—smoking makes sense. That is what TOBACCO: THE DEADLY DRUG is all about.

— *Wade Berrettini MD, PhD*

CHAPTER 1

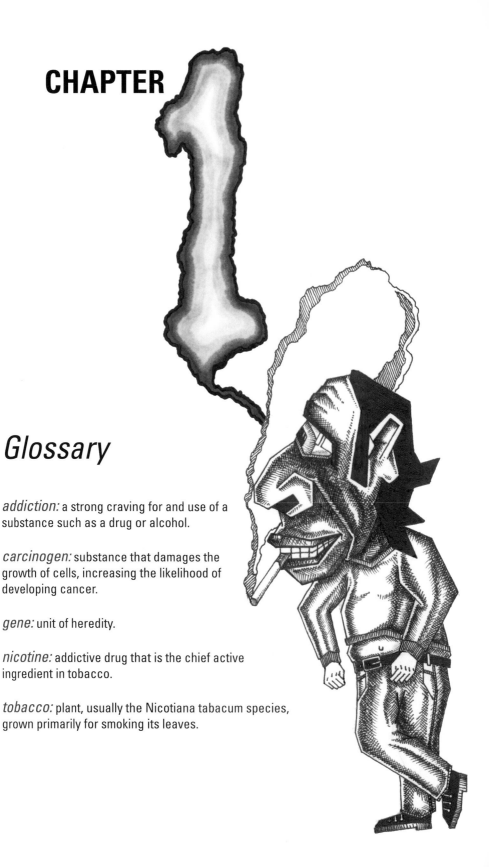

Glossary

addiction: a strong craving for and use of a substance such as a drug or alcohol.

carcinogen: substance that damages the growth of cells, increasing the likelihood of developing cancer.

gene: unit of heredity.

nicotine: addictive drug that is the chief active ingredient in tobacco.

tobacco: plant, usually the Nicotiana tabacum species, grown primarily for smoking its leaves.

The Dangers of Smoking

W. H. is a man in his sixties who appears to be quite healthy. He works a regular schedule, takes care of chores around the house, and generally eats nutritious meals. However, he just had a heart attack. At the hospital, his nurses and doctors have all told him the same thing. He needs to stop smoking.

The Link Between Smoking and Disease

Smoking is a dangerous habit and cigarette smoke can kill. Within *tobacco* smoke are about 4,000 chemical agents. Sixty of them are *carcinogens*, or substances known to cause cancer. Some, such as carbon monoxide, tar, arsenic, and lead, are toxic substances that poison and damage the body, increasing the likelihood of a wide range of other health problems, including heart disease.

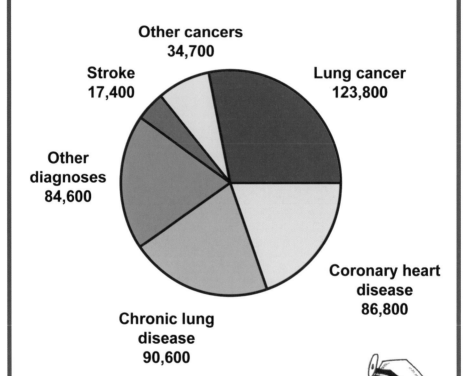

About 438,000 U.S. Deaths Attributable Each Year to Cigarette Smoking*

Other cancers
34,700

Stroke
17,400

Lung cancer
123,800

Other
diagnoses
84,600

Coronary heart
disease
86,800

Chronic lung
disease
90,600

* Average annual number of deaths, 1997–2001.
Source: MMWR 2005;54(25) 625–8

Approximately one out of every five deaths in the United
States each year is directly caused by cigarette smoking
and could have been prevented.

The carcinogens in tobacco smoke make it twenty times more likely that smokers will develop lung cancer than nonsmokers, says the Centers for Disease Control. In fact, cigarette smoking is the cause of the majority of lung cancer deaths in the United States. Smokers are also at greater risk to suffer from cancers in areas that smoke contacts: the mouth, throat, larynx (voice box), and esophagus. Even other parts of the body are at increased risk. Smokers are more likely than nonsmokers to develop cancer of the pancreas, kidney, bladder, and stomach.

Statistics from the Centers for Disease Control and Prevention

- Cancer is the second most common cause of death in the United States.
- Lung cancer is the leading cause of cancer death in both men and women.
- Tobacco use is the leading preventable cause of death in the United States, causing each year approximately 440,000 premature deaths; more than $75 billion in direct medical costs are attributable to smoking.

Smoking is associated with about 30 percent of all deaths from cancer, and close to 90 percent of deaths due to lung cancer. In addition, exposure to the toxins in tobacco smoke is known to increase a person's chance of heart disease, stroke, and respiratory illnesses, including lung diseases such as emphysema and chronic bronchitis.

The relationship between smoking and illness was known as early as 1964, when *The Report of the Surgeon General's Advisory Committee on Smoking and Health* was published. The following year, Congress required cigarette makers to put labels on their products to warn

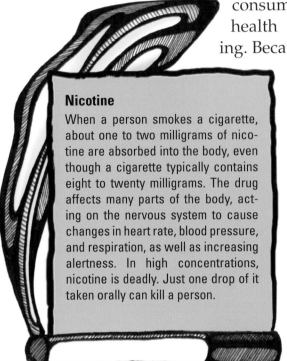

Nicotine

When a person smokes a cigarette, about one to two milligrams of nicotine are absorbed into the body, even though a cigarette typically contains eight to twenty milligrams. The drug affects many parts of the body, acting on the nervous system to cause changes in heart rate, blood pressure, and respiration, as well as increasing alertness. In high concentrations, nicotine is deadly. Just one drop of it taken orally can kill a person.

consumers about the negative health consequences of smoking. Because tobacco use has been linked to disease, disability, and death, the advertising of cigarettes on television and the radio has been banned since September 1970.

Yet for many years, cigarette manufacturers refused to acknowledge the link between smoking and disease. It was not until 1997 that the American tobacco industry agreed to pay $368 billion to forty-six U.S. states, six U.S. territories, and Washington, D.C., as compensation for health-related damages caused to American citizens by cigarette smoke over the years.

Yet, despite the warnings and ever-increasing knowledge that tobacco is dangerous to health, people continue to smoke. Today, nearly one out of every four Americans smokes. According to National Institute on Drug Abuse in the United States, more than 440,000 individuals die each year from smoking-related diseases. That accounts for one out of every five deaths in the United States. Some experts estimate that as many as 3 million people

worldwide die annually due to smoking-related illnesses. It is estimated that in 2030 smoking may contribute to the death each year of as many as 10 million
people around the world.

A person's overall exposure to tobacco smoke during
his or her lifetime will affect the likelihood of developing smoking-related cancers and noncancerous diseases. Research has shown that the more years a someone smokes and the greater the number of cigarettes
smoked, the greater the risk of suffering lung and other
cancers, heart attack, stroke, or chronic lung disease.
However, studies have also shown that smokers who
quit will immediately benefit from a decreased risk of
developing these health issues. In fact, the earlier a person quits, says the National Cancer Institute, the greater
the overall health benefit.

**Trends in cigarette smoking* among 12th graders, by racial/ethnic group
—United States, 1977–1998+**

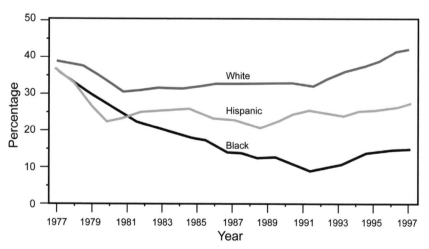

*Smoking on >1 of the 30 days before survey.
+2–year moving averages are used to stabilize estimates.
Source: University of Michigan, Monitoring the Future project.

Despite widespread warnings about the health risks, many people continue to
smoke, including teenagers.

So if the dangers of smoking have been known for so long, why did W. H. and so many other people like him start smoking in the first place? And why don't they stop? W. H. has tried to quit a number of times, but he has never been able to succeed. Why not?

The Power of Nicotine

Smokeless Tobacco

Smokeless tobacco in the form of chewing tobacco also has harmful effects. It can damage gum tissue and even cause the loss of teeth. It also reduces a person's ability to taste and smell. Substances in smokeless tobacco can cause cancers of the mouth, pharynx, larynx, and esophagus. People who develop these cancers typically were users of chewing tobacco.

Despite knowing the dangers of smoking, people continue to smoke because they are addicted to a substance that is naturally present in tobacco—*nicotine*. Nicotine is one of the principal ingredients of any form of tobacco. It is a powerful drug that is quickly absorbed into the bloodstream, traveling to the brain in just seconds. The drug is considered addictive because the user cannot stop using it, and actually requires increasing amounts to create the same effect.

Some experts believe that nicotine is the most addictive drug in the world. It has certainly ensnared more individuals than any other drug. Once they start smoking cigarettes, many people find it extremely difficult to stop. In fact, one out of five American adults, or almost 45 million people, are smokers. Surveys show that about 70 percent of them have tried to quit smoking at some time in their lives. Of those who want to quit smoking, however, fewer than 10 percent ever succeed. Out of every 100 smokers, only 7 succeed in quitting.

Because of the terrible health risks of smoking and the cost to society, public health advocates, medical professionals, and researchers are all searching for ways to combat nicotine *addiction* and help people break the smoking habit. They try to understand the reasons some people who start smoking are able to quit while others struggle endlessly to stop. What is it that separates the "successful quitters" from the lifelong smokers?

Scientists and therapists believe that several factors, such as peer pressure, stress, and a lack of willpower, explain why people begin using tobacco. These same influences deter users who are trying to quit. However,

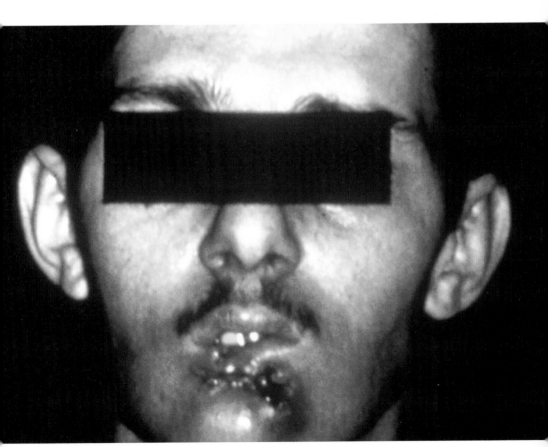

Mouth cancer is one of the possible harmful effects of smokeless tobacco.

Just as eye color and hair type are determined by a person's genes, addiction to nicotine may also have a genetic component.

although these factors may play a role in the problem of nicotine use, they are only parts of the smoking puzzle. In recent years, science and newly emerging technologies have brought to light another possible explanation for differences between smokers and nonsmokers, and between quitters and nonquitters—genetics.

What Is Genetics?

Genetics is the branch of biology that deals with heredity—the way that qualities and traits are passed on from parent to child. A person's individual *genes*, or units of heredity, determine specific traits. For example, a girl has blue eyes and curly hair because she received genes from at least one of his or her parents that held genetic information determining blue eyes and wavy hair.

Some scientists believe that the genetic information carried in genes of some people make them more likely to use tobacco or become addicted to nicotine. To confirm this theory, investigators have tried to gain a better understanding of the biological aspects of substance dependence and addiction and its impact on the brain.

Scientists have found evidence that genetics can play a role in several aspects of smoking, affecting whether people begin to smoke in the first place and if current smokers can successfully quit. Research in nicotine addiction offers one of the most promising avenues of investigation in the search for new therapies to help smokers quit the habit or prevent them from starting.

CHAPTER

Glossary

dopamine: a neurotransmitter present in regions of the brain that affects the perception of pain and pleasure.

molecule: the smallest physical unit of a substance that can exist independently.

neurotransmitter: a brain chemical that carries signals or information from one nerve cell to another.

receptor: a part of a nerve cell that responds to a specific neurotransmitter.

tolerance: adaptation resulting from continued use of a drug so that greater amounts are needed to achieve the same response.

withdrawal: process of ceasing chronic use of an addictive drug.

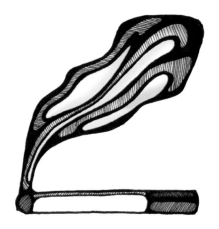

Understanding Nicotine Addiction

Ben stood on his back porch with his friend Luke, grilling burgers and enjoying the warm summer evening. Feeling a desire to smoke, Ben pulled out a crumpled, nearly empty pack of cigarettes. He drew one from the pack and bent down over the grill to light it.

"Be careful," Luke cautioned, watching him worriedly. "You're going to burn yourself."

"I'll be fine," Ben replied. "I do this all the time."

"All the time, huh? Maybe that's a sign you should think about quitting. I mean, quitting for real this time." Luke often teased Ben about his smoking habit. Ben knew Luke did this

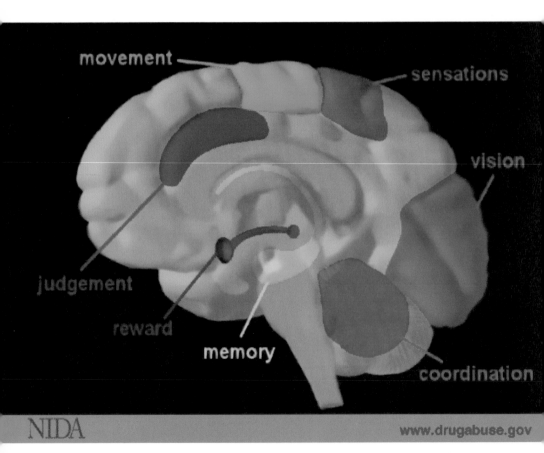

for his own good, and it didn't bother him. He pulled up from the grill and blew a thin stream of smoke out the side of his mouth.

"I could quit anytime I want," he declared. "I just don't want to."

"That's the most overused line ever," Luke replied. "Don't tell me you actually believe it."

"No," Ben said, taking the cigarette from his mouth and staring at it for a moment. "No, I don't actually believe it," came his quiet reply. "But it's easier than admitting that I'm a slave to nicotine."

The reward pathway in the brain remembers an activity that is pleasurable, such as smoking, and as a result a person will have a physiological desire to repeat the activity.

Understanding Addiction

Addiction is a condition in which a person craves a substance and is unable to stop using it. Someone who knows that smoking is unhealthy yet still continues to smoke a pack of cigarettes a day is an addict.

To people who are not addicted, the behavior of someone who is struggling with an addiction may look odd and irrational. The inability to quit may seem as though there is a weakness of will on the part of the individual. However, the grip of addictive substances can be very strong and very subtle. Many times people don't even realize they are addicted. They are unaware that their continuous use of an addictive substance has brought about changes in the wiring of their brain.

Natural Reward Pathways

Within the human brain is a complex network of reward pathways, which are a part of the brain circuitry. When a person experiences pleasurable feelings, such as eating or sharing company with family and friends, the reward pathway in the brain is activated. The person feels good and wants to repeat the activity that brought pleasure. Scientists believe that the existence of reward pathways motivated primitive peoples to seek out food and companionship that helped ensure their survival.

An important part of the reward circuitry is a set of nerve cells (called neurons) known as the ventral tegmental area, or VTA, which is located near the base of

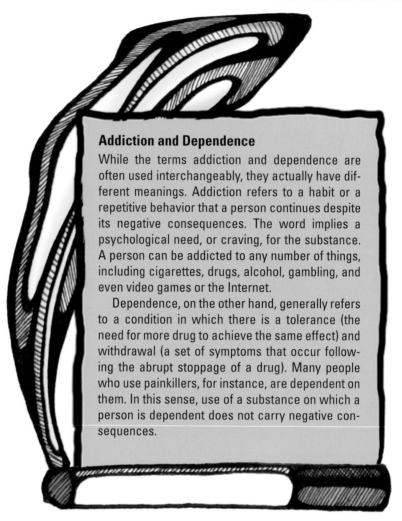

Addiction and Dependence

While the terms addiction and dependence are often used interchangeably, they actually have different meanings. Addiction refers to a habit or a repetitive behavior that a person continues despite its negative consequences. The word implies a psychological need, or craving, for the substance. A person can be addicted to any number of things, including cigarettes, drugs, alcohol, gambling, and even video games or the Internet.

Dependence, on the other hand, generally refers to a condition in which there is a tolerance (the need for more drug to achieve the same effect) and withdrawal (a set of symptoms that occur following the abrupt stoppage of a drug). Many people who use painkillers, for instance, are dependent on them. In this sense, use of a substance on which a person is dependent does not carry negative consequences.

the brain. The neurons in the VTA communicate with other parts of the brain by producing special chemicals, or *neurotransmitters*, that carry signals. There are more than 100 neurotransmitters in the brain that carry messages throughout the nervous system. The neurotransmitter *dopamine* is an essential part of the reward circuitry.

When the neuron cells in the VTA are stimulated, dopamine is released. The signal passes from one nerve cell to another across a small space called a synapse, until reaching neurons in the nucleus accumbens. This structure is located in the prefrontal cortex, near the front of the brain.

The nerve cells in the nucleus accumbens have special binding sites, called *receptors*, which respond to specific neurotransmitters. Receptors are much like locks that open only when a brain chemical of the proper size and shape comes into contact with them. When the appropriate neurotransmitter binds to the receptor to activate it, the cell will take a certain action. This action varies depending on the type of receptor. The dopamine molecule latches onto the dopamine receptor and sends its signal into the cell, which in turn causes the body to register a pleasurable sensation.

While other parts of the brain help determine whether or not an experience is pleasurable, and whether it should be repeated or avoided, the VTA-accumbens pathway determines how rewarding the experience is. If an activity is very pleasurable, the organism will then remember and have a physiological desire to repeat it.

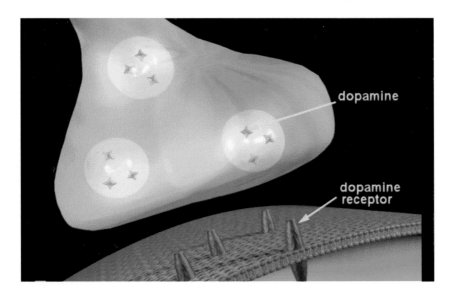

The dopamine molecule latches onto the dopamine receptor and sends its signal into the cell.

Neurons produce special chemicals, or neurotransmitters, that carry messages throughout the nervous system.

This same pleasurable sensation is what can cause people to have trouble stopping themselves from eating a whole bag of potato chips or cookies at once. Few people stop after eating just one chip or cookie, unless they make a conscious effort to do so. This is because the brain reward pathway registers the sensation of eating that particular food as pleasurable, and so the body wants more.

Drug Reward Pathways

The dopamine pathway from the VTA to the nucleus accumbens plays an important role in addiction. Researchers have found that addictive drugs like nicotine are able to take over the natural reward circuit system in the brain.

Nicotine enters the bloodstream through the lungs if tobacco is smoked, or if it is sniffed or chewed, the

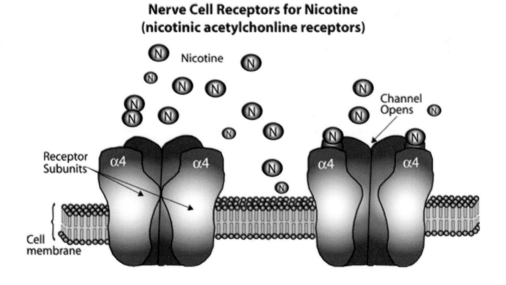

Nerve Cell Receptors for Nicotine
(nicotinic acetylchonline receptors)

Because the nicotine molecule has a similar structure to that of acetylcholine, nicotine attaches to receptors normally used by acetylcholine.

nicotine passes through the mucous membranes of the mouth or nose. Once in the bloodstream, the drug is rapidly dispersed throughout the body. Within 10 seconds, it reaches the brain, and nicotine *molecules* attach to receptors normally used by the neurotransmitter acetylcholine. Because the nicotine molecule has a similar structure to that of acetylcholine, nicotine binds at and activates cholinergic receptors, also known as nicotinic acetylcholine receptors. These neurons then release large amounts of dopamine in the nucleus accumbens.

When the nucleus accumbens is flooded with increased levels of dopamine, the smoker experiences intense feelings of pleasure, which is what many smokers call the "kick" or "high" of nicotine. Because the experience of nicotine registers in the brain as rewarding and pleasurable, the brain will want more.

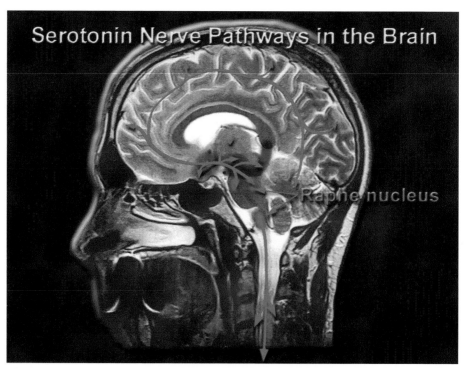

Studies have shown that nicotine slows the passage of serotonin, a calming hormone, through the chemical pathways of the brain.

Changes in the Brain

Nicotine stimulation typically lasts only about 40 to 60 minutes. Soon afterward, the user feels depressed and fatigued. In order to regain the feeling experienced during smoking or chewing tobacco, the user may continue to dose him or herself throughout the day. As the brain becomes accustomed to increased levels of dopamine, it actually begins to change physically. To adjust to too much dopamine, the brain reduces the amount of the neurotransmitter and number of its receptors.

These changes in the brain mean the nicotine user is developing *tolerance* to the nicotine. To achieve the body's normal levels of dopamine, he or she must now regularly supply the brain with nicotine. The developing tolerance to nicotine also means that the same amount of the drug has a reduced effect. To get the same amount of pleasure from smoking, the addicted person will need to smoke more cigarettes than before. If levels of the drug drop, the user will feel irritable and depressed.

And if the addicted smoker tries to stop using nicotine altogether, the changes that have already occurred in the brain will cause problems. Without the accustomed levels of dopamine and nicotine in the brain, the body will suffer the symptoms of *withdrawal*—that is, the withdrawal of nicotine.

Withdrawal is an unpleasant experience in which the body craves the substance the person has become addicted to. If this craving is not met, the nicotine-addicted person may feel symptoms of physical sickness—

Withdrawal from nicotine can make a person feel tired, anxious, and irritable.

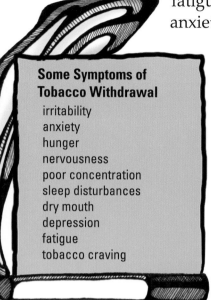

Some Symptoms of Tobacco Withdrawal

irritability
anxiety
hunger
nervousness
poor concentration
sleep disturbances
dry mouth
depression
fatigue
tobacco craving

fatigue, irritability, insomnia, anxiety, headache, and other similarly unpleasant sensations. These symptoms can last for just a few weeks or up to several months. Even after a person has stopped using nicotine, the desire for the drug can reoccur, often in response to habitual times when the individual would reach for a cigarette or chewing tobacco.

Because nicotine rewires the reward system in the brain, it is an addictive substance. It alters brain function in the same way that addictive drugs like cocaine or heroin do. Studies show that the pull of nicotine is so strong that most addicted people who are trying to quit typically stop trying within a week's time. The desire for nicotine dominates the addicted person's behavior so much that he or she will find it is extremely difficult to quit.

Learning how the brain works is important to understanding nicotine's addictive hold on those who use tobacco products. As research on addiction continues, scientists may be able to gain a better understanding of how to identify individuals in danger of becoming addicted and how to assist those struggling to control their addictions.

CHAPTER 3

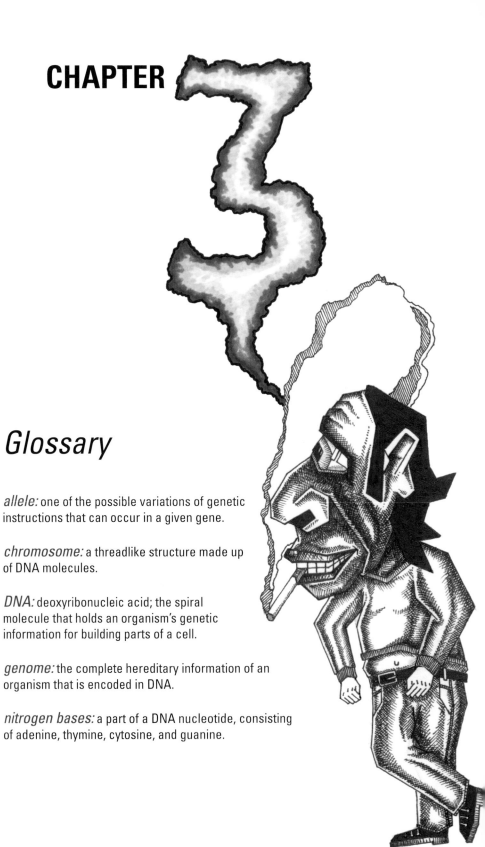

Glossary

allele: one of the possible variations of genetic instructions that can occur in a given gene.

chromosome: a threadlike structure made up of DNA molecules.

DNA: deoxyribonucleic acid; the spiral molecule that holds an organism's genetic information for building parts of a cell.

genome: the complete hereditary information of an organism that is encoded in DNA.

nitrogen bases: a part of a DNA nucleotide, consisting of adenine, thymine, cytosine, and guanine.

The Basics
of Genetics

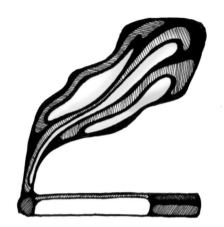

On the popular television show *Heroes*, Dr. Mohinder Suresh uses a complicated mathematical formula to locate individuals with amazing powers. In the show, some of the characters can fly, read minds, or heal wounds. These superpowers supposedly result from subtle, yet fateful, changes in the heroes' genes. While the idea of superheroes developing because of gene mutations is entertaining, the concept is more science fiction than science fact.

As units of heredity, genes don't influence superhero abilities. But they are very important in helping to determine who a person is and how his or her body will develop and

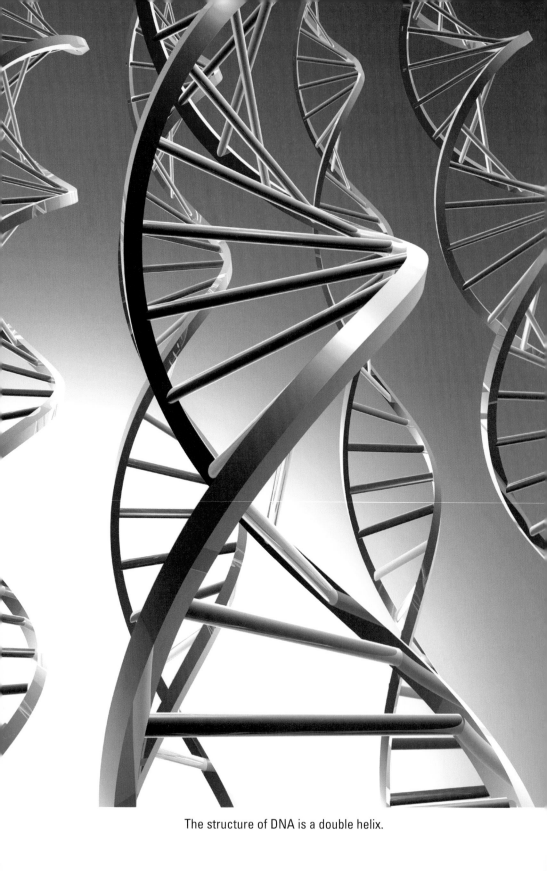

The structure of DNA is a double helix.

function. The instructions contained in genes provide information for cells that allow an organism to develop, function, and reproduce. Genes carry the genetic information that affects a person's physical characteristics, such as hair color, skin color, eye color, and height. Genes also play a role in the development of certain behaviors, such as instincts, and in predisposition to disease.

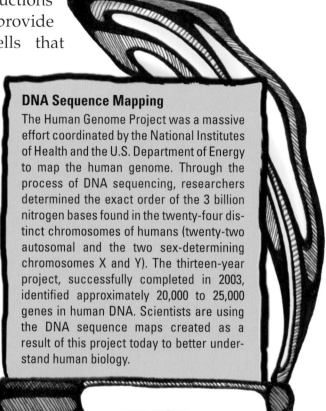

DNA Sequence Mapping

The Human Genome Project was a massive effort coordinated by the National Institutes of Health and the U.S. Department of Energy to map the human genome. Through the process of DNA sequencing, researchers determined the exact order of the 3 billion nitrogen bases found in the twenty-four distinct chromosomes of humans (twenty-two autosomal and the two sex-determining chromosomes X and Y). The thirteen-year project, successfully completed in 2003, identified approximately 20,000 to 25,000 genes in human DNA. Scientists are using the DNA sequence maps created as a result of this project today to better understand human biology.

DNA

The genetic information encoded in genes begins with *DNA*, which is short for deoxyribonucleic acid. DNA is the molecule that carries the body's genetic information. It is like a set of blueprints, storing information needed to construct other parts of cells.

Graphic representations or models of the DNA molecule reveal a structure that looks like a tightly spiraling ladder. In these models, two long ribbons twist in a spiral, forming a double helix shape.

The DNA molecule consists of millions of nucleotides that are linked together. These nucleotides have three parts: a phosphate group, a sugar group, and one of four types of *nitrogen bases*. The sides of the double helix are the phosphates and sugars. Attached to each sugar at regular intervals are the nitrogen bases, which fit into each other like pieces of a puzzle. There are just four kinds of nitrogen bases in nucleotides. They are adenine, thymine, cytosine, and guanine—usually represented as the letters A, T, C, and G.

Unlocking the Secrets of DNA

James Watson and Francis Crick are credited with discovering in 1953 that the structure of DNA is a double helix, but much of their work was based on X-ray data collected by Rosalind Franklin. Maurice Wilkins, one of Franklin's colleagues, showed James Watson Franklin's X-ray diffraction photograph of DNA without her permission. Watson reported that after seeing the photograph, he immediately recognized that the DNA structure was the double helix.

In 1962, Watson, Crick, and Wilkins were awarded a Nobel Prize for their discovery. Rosalind Franklin, having died of ovarian cancer in 1957, did not share in the recognition.

The bases always match up in pairs, in a way that forms the steps of a spiral DNA ladder. Each base always matches up with the same partner. If the sugar on one side of the DNA molecule has a C, then the sugar on the other side will always have a G. Simi-

larly, C binds together only with G. It is the sequence, or order, of these four bases that encodes specific genetic information, much like letters of the alphabet form words and sentences when placed in a certain order.

Genes, Proteins, and Chromosomes

The segments of DNA that carry specific coded information are called genes. The coded instructions in genes

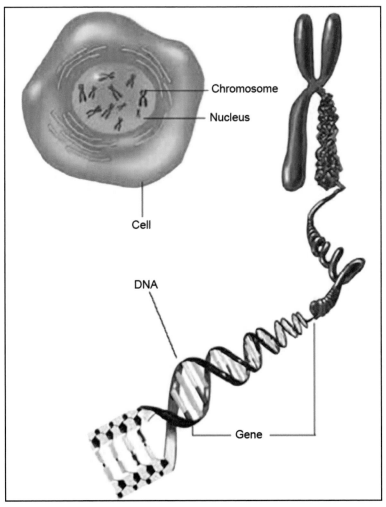

The DNA molecule is tightly coiled and packed in a chromosome.

tell cells how to produce proteins, which in turn direct the activities of cells and functions of the body. Within each of the 100 trillion cells found in the human body are thousands of different proteins that work together to help each individual cell perform specific functions.

The long threadlike DNA molecule is tightly coiled and packed in a chromosome. Most of the genetic material of a cell, in the form of chromosomes can be found in the membrane-enclosed cell nucleus. Each human cell contains 46 chromosomes, organized into twenty-three pairs. There are twenty-two autosomal (nonsex) chromosomes and two chromosomes that determine the sex of an organism. Half of a person's chromosomes come from the mother and half from the father. A person's complete hereditary information, called the *genome*, is encoded in DNA.

Genes and Alleles

All humans share the same basic set of genes, arranged in the same order. This means that specific genes that

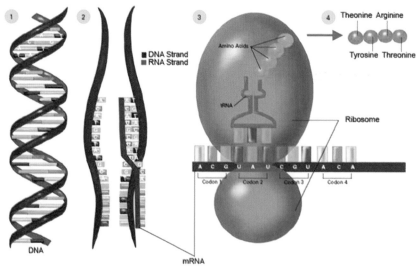

All of a person's hereditary information, called the *genome*, is encoded in DNA.

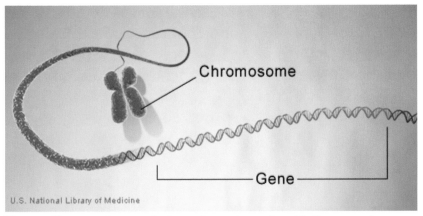

Chromosome

Gene

U.S. National Library of Medicine

The specific genes for a particular trait are always found in the same place on a DNA strand.

determine a particular trait are always found in the same place, or locus, of a DNA strand. For example, the instructions that determine the size of an individual's feet occupy the same DNA locus. Whether a person has big feet or little feet, narrow feet or wide feet, the genetic instructions for making feet of these sizes and shapes are stored in the same place.

People come in a variety of shapes, colors, and sizes, so genes come in various forms, called *alleles*, that contain the specific instructions for these different traits. An allele is simply one form, or variant, of genetic instructions found in a particular gene. A gene can contain many possible variations of instructions from several alleles. For example, one allele might have instructions for the trait of blond hair and another for brown hair.

Different alleles do not change the fundamental nature of an organism; they only change traits. A boy with green eyes is different from a boy with brown eyes, for example, but not so much that the two are classified as different kinds of organisms. All humans actually share 99.9 percent identical DNA.

Mendel

In the mid-1800s, an Austrian monk named Gregor Mendel spent several years breeding pea plants and carefully recording information about the inheritance of their specific traits. Ultimately, Mendel came up with theories of heredity, known as the Laws of Inheritance, that geneticists still use today. Because of his pioneering contributions to the field, Mendel is known today as the father of genetics.

Like Father, Like Son?

In simplest terms, a person's genetic information consists of the characteristics and traits inherited from his or her parents. Because each human has two sets of chromosomes, he or she usually has two alleles with the potential to influence a specific trait. Each parent passes one of these alleles to their offspring. The child will then have two alleles—one from the mother and one from the father.

The presence of alleles explains how a red-haired boy can have two blond parents. If both the mother and father each had an allele for red air and another for blond, both parents could pass on an allele for red hair.

However, if both parents had the red-hair allele to begin with, why didn't they also have red hair?

The answer is that when two alleles encoded for different traits occur (in this case, one for red hair and one for blond hair), they interact. In many cases, one allele is dominant over the other, which means that only its

Condition affecting members of a family

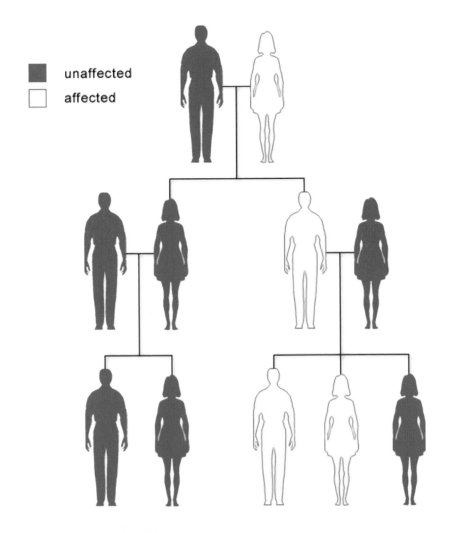

The conditions we inherit from our parents depend on which alleles they pass on to us.

instructions are followed. The dominant allele masks the recessive allele. For example, in the case of the red-haired boy's parents, both his mother and father had genes in which the blond allele was dominant. However, they both carried recessive alleles for red hair. These recessive alleles were paired in their son, and the genetic instructions of the two recessive alleles resulted in the development of the boy's red hair.

Sometimes the interaction between allele pairs is additive, which is to say that their effects add up. In people, additive alleles occur with the traits like skin color. A wide range of skin colors exists in humans because the alleles that code for skin color work together in an additive fashion. Although the genetic instructions still remain separate and distinct, colors encoded in the alleles blend together. As a result, the daughter of a very dark-skinned mother and a light-skinned father may have skin that is almost any shade between the two, depending on the alleles she inherits from her parents.

Because each parent passes along only one allele from each gene pair randomly, the twenty-three chromosomes inherited from each parent combine to form a unique set

Punnett Squares

One way to understand how genes are passed from parents to children is by diagramming it. A Punnett square is a simple tool for representing all the possible combinations of alleles that can occur when two organisms reproduce. The diagram looks a bit like a multiplication table that uses letters instead of numbers. One parent's alleles go along the top, and the other parent's alleles go along the side. (Uppercase letters indicate dominant alleles and lowercase indicate recessive ones.) The possible combinations of alleles appear in the center boxes of the square.

of traits for the child. The existence of recessive alleles allows for certain traits to remain hidden in parents or grandparents, only to appear in their children. This is how a red-haired child can result from the union of two blond-haired parents. Recessive alleles also explains how a person with albinism—a trait in which there is no melanin pigment in the eyes, skin, and hair—can have parents without this trait. The mixing and matching of alleles is why children can be like their parents in some ways and unlike them in others.

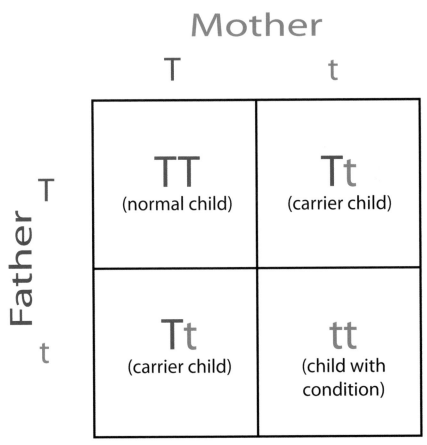

A Punnett square is a diagram used to show all the possible combinations of alleles that can result when two organisms reproduce.

Patterns of Inheritance

The traits discussed thus far have largely been those determined by a pattern of inheritance known as simple, or monogenic, inheritance. The prefix *mono* means "one," and the root word *genic* refers to genes. Simple or monogenic inheritance is fairly uncomplicated because it involves only two alleles from a single gene. The alleles of that gene have total control over how that trait will be built. Few observable traits are governed by only one gene, however, although thousands of unseen traits,

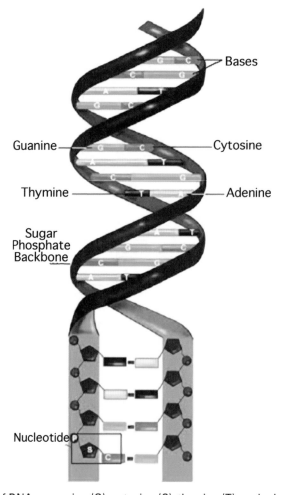

The bases of DNA—guanine (G), cytosine (C), thymine (T), and adenine (A)—are found in pairs that make up the rungs of the DNA ladder.

including a great many inherited diseases, are determined by monogenic inheritance.

More common is complex, or polygenic inheritance. This describes a pattern of instructions that involves the alleles contained in multiple genes. Most of the time, traits are shaped by more than one gene.

Genetic Testing

If the genetic instructions in a gene mutate, it make not make the specified protein or the protein itself could be altered. Abnormal or damaged genes may not be able to direct the building of proteins that help the body perform a specific function. Researchers have found that gene mutations or the lack of certain genes can indicate the existence or the risk of developing various medical conditions or diseases. Gene mutations may be inherited or they can be caused by a combination of genetic and environmental factors.

Advancements in scientific technology have led to the development of tests in which human DNA, chromosomes, and proteins can be analyzed. More than 1000 kinds of genetic tests currently exist. They are used to help physicians and researchers screen newborns for disease, diagnose whether a person has a disease, or predict the probability of the individual developing or passing along certain diseases and conditions to his or her children. Some inherited diseases for which genetic testing currently exists include cystic fibrosis, Huntington's disease, sickle cell disease, and Tay-Sachs disease.

In genetic testing, DNA is extracted from a sample such as blood, hair, or skin. Then the order of the nucleotide bases in the DNA segment is determined, or sequenced. Technicians evaluate the results, looking for specific changes in chromosomes, DNA, or proteins, depending on the suspected disorder.

Geneticists—scientists who study heredity and variations of inherited characteristics—also use genetic testing in research. For example, when trying to identify the gene or genes that carry instructions for certain traits

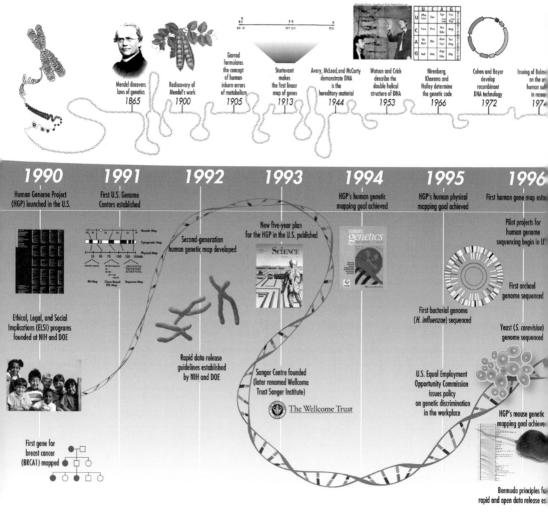

A history of genetics and the Human Genome Project (HGP).

or specific conditions, researchers will look for similar alleles when comparing DNA sequences of people with the same conditions.

Tools like genetic testing allow researchers to gain a better understand of the role that specific alleles play in the complex biological and chemical systems of the body.

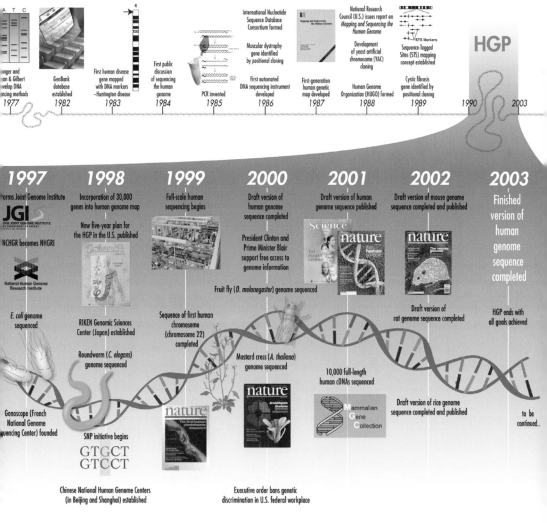

Types of mutation

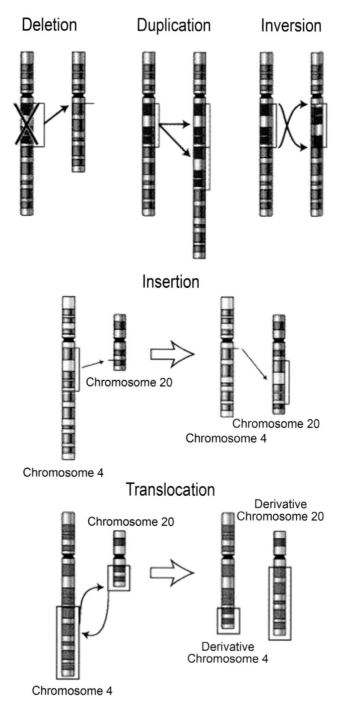

Gene mutations or the lack of certain genes can indicate the existence of or the risk of developing certain medical conditions or diseases.

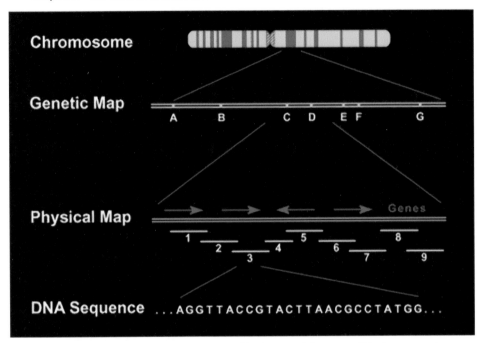

Geneticists use genetic mapping to identify the gene(s) responsible for a certain disease or trait.

Scientists have already identified many genes that affect specific diseases and conditions. But because more than 20,000 genes can be found in human DNA, much remains to be done.

CHAPTER 4

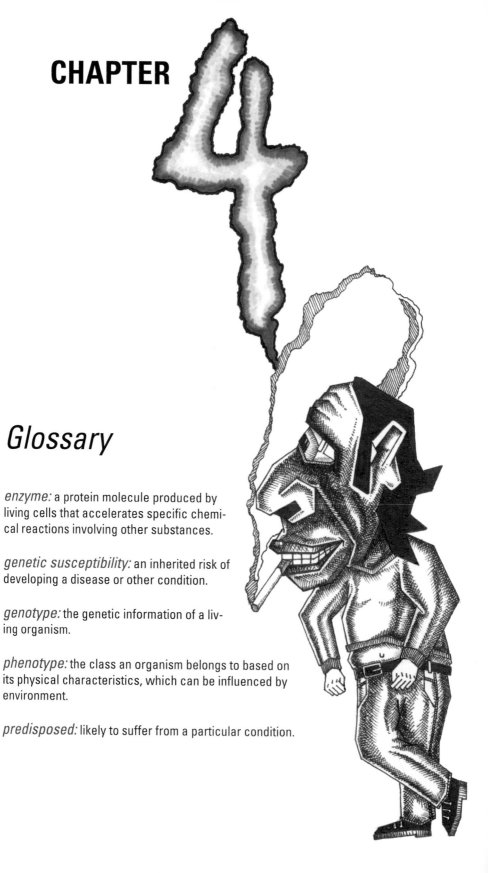

Glossary

enzyme: a protein molecule produced by living cells that accelerates specific chemical reactions involving other substances.

genetic susceptibility: an inherited risk of developing a disease or other condition.

genotype: the genetic information of a living organism.

phenotype: the class an organism belongs to based on its physical characteristics, which can be influenced by environment.

predisposed: likely to suffer from a particular condition.

A Genetic Connection

At twenty-two years old, Thomas is in pretty good shape, having played several sports throughout high school and college. But when his father had a heart attack recently, Thomas became worried that he wasn't doing enough. While visiting his father in the hospital, Thomas overheard a conversation between one of the nurses and his father.

"Is there anyone else in your family who has ever had a heart attack?" the nurse asked.

"Yes," Thomas's father replied. "My father and grandfather both had heart attacks when they were fairly young. My father actually had more than one." The nurse wrote something down on her clipboard before speaking again.

"Well, heart attacks often run in families," she said. "Tell me about your smoking, diet, and exercise patterns."

Thomas didn't pay much attention to the subsequent conversation. He was thinking about his own chances of having a heart attack. If heart attacks run in the family, and his father, grandfather, and great-grandfather had all had them, he thought, how could he hope to avoid having one, too? Thomas had already inherited his father's red hair and freckles. Surely something in his genome was just ticking away toward a heart attack. After all, he thought, you can't change your genes.

Other Influences

If Thomas had listened further, however, he might have heard the nurse talk about how diet, exercise, medication use, and lifestyle habits—in addition to genetics—can affect a person's chance of having a heart attack. And he might have learned that an individual's genetic makeup does not guarantee a specific outcome. Although a medical history or genetic tests can indicate a likelihood of disease in a family, sometimes, a person's genetic makeup only provides clues about his or her health risks.

Interacting with genes are factors such as the environment (where a person lives or works) and behavior (diet and exercise patterns). By changing aspects in environment or behavior, a person can affect whether or not a protein encoded by a gene is produced, or expressed. Gene expression occurs when the encoded instructions in the gene are carried out and help to produce a specific trait. However, certain conditions can prevent a gene's instructions from being carried out.

A smoker at risk of developing heart disease—that is, someone whose family history suggests that he or she is *predisposed* to having a heart attack—can improve the

A person's genetic makeup provides clues about his or her health risks, but it's not the whole story.

Autosomal Recessive Inheritance

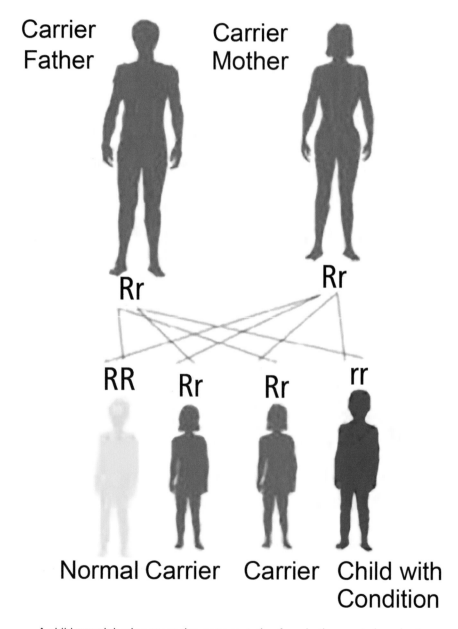

Carrier Father

Carrier Mother

Rr

Rr

RR Rr Rr rr

Normal Carrier Carrier Child with Condition

A child must inherit a recessive gene mutation from both parents in order to have the disease caused by the mutation.

odds of staying healthy by eating a nutritious diet, getting regular exercise, and dropping the nicotine habit. Studies have shown that changing the environment and behavior can reduce a person's odds suffering from heart disease.

Genotype and Phenotype

An important concept for scientists working in genetics is the distinction between the genetic information of an organism and the actual observable, physical traits that an organism has. If a gene is not expressed, an organism may exhibit traits that would normally occur according to its genetic makeup. Scientists use the terms *genotype* and *phenotype* to indicate this difference: Genotype refers to the actual genetic makeup, or genome, of a living organism, which may or may not be expressed. Phenotype refers to the actual physical traits that can be seen, and which can often be influenced by the environment.

Geneticists describe the genetic makeup, or genotype, of a pea plant in the following way: Its dominant allele for purple flowers is signified by an uppercase "P" and its recessive allele for white flowers is represented with a lowercase "p." Thus, the genotype of the plant would be "Pp." This describes the actual alleles present in the plant's genetic makeup.

In looking at the plant, one can see that it has purple flowers. This description of the plant's physical trait—the flower color is purple—is the plant's phenotype. In this case, the phenotype is the same as would be expected according to the organism's genetic instructions.

Although genetic information can control a phenotype, outside influences sometimes prevent gene expression and cause a phenotype to differ from what would be expected according to the genotype. For example, if a flamingo eats a certain kind of shrimp, it will have pink feathers even though the bird's genetic information, or genotype, indicates the feathers should be white. In another illustration, a boy may be born with the genetic information to be six feet tall. However, if he is malnourished while he is growing up, he may reach only five feet in height. Without proper nutrition, his body simply can't grow to its full potential.

Nature and Nurture

Long before genetics became a formal branch of science, before anybody even knew the principles of genetics, philosophers pondered the question of nature versus nurture. That is, are people born with a personality, appearance, and set of talents— as determined by nature? Or are they shaped by their experiences and the influences of the world around them—by how they have been nurtured?

As science has advanced knowledge about the workings of the human brain and body, the question of nature versus nurture has also evolved. For geneticists, the question has become: To what extent does a person's genetic makeup determine how that individual will develop, and to what extent does environment determine how a person's genetic makeup is translated?

Genetic Destiny

Some traits cannot be changed, regardless of environmental influences. Certain characteristics such as eye color are not affected by outside factors. This is also true of some traits that are not visible, such as inherited diseases or other health conditions. For instance, if a daughter receives the recessive albinism allele from each of her

Humans have long pondered the question of nature vs. nurture.

parents, then her body will not be able to produce melanin pigment in the eyes, skin, and hair. Similarly, a boy will develop sickle cell anemia if he inherits the recessive allele for the disease from both from his mother and father. No amount of environmental influence can change these conditions.

When a certain trait, such as a sickle cell disease or blue eyes, is determined solely by a person's genome, the outcome can be said to constitute the person's genetic destiny. The genetic makeup of a person does not necessarily determine what traits that person will have. Certain genes or their lack can, however, indicate that a person is susceptible to certain conditions.

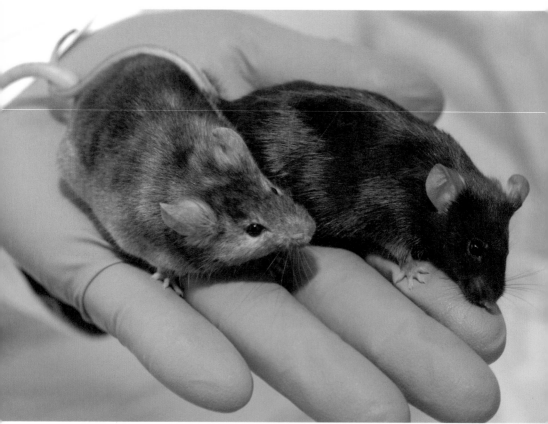

Mice, which are fairly intelligent animals, are often used in genetic research.

Genetic Susceptibility

Genetic susceptibility refers to when a person's genetic makeup puts him or her at risk of developing a condition or disease. For example, studies have shown that individuals with lung cancer are more likely to be missing the gene GSTM1 than people without the disease. GSTM1 is responsible for producing an *enzyme* that reduces the toxicity of environmental carcinogens found in cigarette smoke. Through genetic testing, in this case a simple blood test, a smoker can determine whether or not she is missing this gene. If the individual is lacking the gene, he or she is considered at increased risk to lung cancer.

Studying Nicotine Use and Addiction

Because addiction affects the dopamine reward pathway, some genetic research has focused on various aspects of the biological and chemical processes that occur in the brain when a person uses nicotine. For example, a study may examine whether a particular allele plays a role in clearing nicotine from the body. Other researchers may study other aspects of a person's body chemistry. For instance, investigators may try to identify the allele that affects how a person perceives the taste of tobacco.

There are a variety of ways to study nicotine and learn about its effect on the body. In conducting their investigations, researchers use several methodologies.

Animal Studies

One common method for studying specific genes is to experiment on animals that have been genetically modified to serve as ideal test specimens. Researchers breed animals—usually mice—that have the exact mix of alleles the researchers want to examine. The animals are then exposed to a variety of conditions and experiments, and their behaviors or physical reactions are observed and recorded.

Researchers interested in the genes involved in nicotine addiction may experiment with the drug on mice that have been bred to have a particular mix of alleles. Because mice are fairly intelligent animals, they are often used in experiments in which they learn how to use a simple mechanism to dose themselves with nicotine. Scientists observe the behavior of the mice, recording information on how often they self dose as well as other actions. By comparing the behavior of groups of mice with different alleles, researchers can form certain hypotheses as to the effects of those specific alleles appear to have on the nicotine-usage habits of the mice.

One advantage of animal studies is that they do not threaten the life or health of human subjects. Ethically, no researcher would be allowed to use human subjects in an experiment in which these subjects might suffer serious health consequences. Another advantage is that mice can reproduce very quickly, allowing researchers to test their theories many times at little cost.

The major disadvantage of this study design, however, is that while mice have many of the same genes as humans, they are different organisms. Thus, conclusions drawn from these kinds of studies might not apply in people.

Population Studies

In the population study, researchers evaluate a very large group of subjects, identifying those affected by a specific condition and those who are not. Investigators then use genetic testing to look for look for similarities in genetic makeup among those affected by the particular condition and for differences among those without the condition.

For example, in evaluating the role of certain alleles in nicotine addiction, researchers may identify a particular allele in a large percentage of the addicted group. And investigators might also see that a very low percentage of the nonaddicted group have that allele. As a result of their findings, the researchers may conclude that the allele in question plays some kind of role in causing nicotine addiction.

Population studies avoid the major problem with animal studies because the data obtained come directly

Population studies allow researchers to look for similarities in genetic makeup among people affected by a certain condition.

The advantage of population studies over animal studies is that the data obtained come directly from humans.

from humans rather than from animals. On the other hand, population studies do not provide clues about why a given allele may have the effect the researchers observed. In addition, other factors that might influence the findings must be taken into consideration when interpreting the data from a population study.

Twin Studies

One of the most effective ways of determining whether genetics influence a health condition is to study that condition in twins, particularly identical twins. Because identical twins have developed from the same egg and sperm, they have the same genetic makeup. Any differences between them are often due to the influence of environmental factors. Investigators study hundreds of sets of twins, looking to identify shared characteristics or qualities.

Researchers interested in determining the influence of genetics on nicotine addiction and smoking habits will compare twins who smoke and those who do not smoke. This study design is extremely valuable because it allows investigators to distinguish between genetic influences and environmental influences on both diseases and conditions such as addictions.

And the Research Says . . .

Based on twin studies of cigarette smoking, researchers have estimated that the heritability of starting to smoke (smoking initiation) is 50 percent and of continuing to smoke (smoking persistence) is 70 percent. Heritability refers likelihood of a trait being passed from one generation to the next. In other words, a person whose family members are habitual smokers has a genetic predisposition to becoming a smoker, too. Studies show that inherited characteristics accounts for about half of his or her risk of becoming a habitual smoker.

While some research has shown the existence of specific genes that could predict an increased risk of nicotine addiction, scientists believe that many genes are involved in both smoking initiation and smoking persistence. Still, much more research needs to be done in order to identify these genes. It does appear that some people have a genetic makeup that predisposes them to nicotine addiction, while others are more likely to be able to quit once they've begun smoking.

The genetic tendency to become a smoker will amount to nothing if the person never begins smoking in the first place. If a person who is genetically susceptible to nicotine addiction is never exposed to cigarettes or any other form of tobacco, there is no way the individual

Scientists believe that many genes are involved in both smoking initiation and nicotine dependence.

Studies of identical twins, whose genetic makeup is the same, make it possible to distinguish between genetic and environmental influences on conditions such as addictions.

can become addicted to it. Studies have shown that the younger the smoker is when he or she begins, the harder it will be for the nicotine user to stop.

Research has shown that a person can have a genetic susceptibility to becoming a smoker or to developing a nicotine addiction, or both. Someday, genetic research on smoking may help people learn whether they carry genes that indicate a predisposition to smoke, to become addicted, or have a hard time trying to quit.

CHAPTER

Glossary

hormone: a chemical that circulates in the bloodstream and regulates cell and tissue activity.

metabolism: the chemical processes by which substances are broken down into energy or other forms for use by a cell or organism.

pathological: relating to disease.

Body Chemistry

Many chemical interactions take place in the body when a person lights up a cigarette and inhales the smoke. Smoking as a single action may not be all that difficult, but the chemical interactions that take place in the body in forming a nicotine addiction are complex.

The introduction of nicotine into the body changes its normal chemistry. In addition to the effects on the dopamine reward pathway of the brain, the drug is known to affect the levels of certain *hormones*. Hormone are chemicals produced by glands in the body. They circulate in the bloodstream and affect and regulate cell and tissue activity.

Hormone Levels

When nicotine enters the bloodstream, it stimulates the release of the hormone adrenaline from the adrenal glands, which are located on top of the kidneys. Adrenaline causes the sudden release of glucose (a natural sugar) in the bloodstream, constricts blood vessels, and increases blood pressure, the rate of respiration, and heart rate.

Nicotine also promotes the release of beta-endorphin, a hormone produced in the pituitary gland, located at the base of the brain. This hormone is associated with blocking the sensation of pain.

At the same time that adrenaline is causing an increase of sugar in the body, nicotine is affecting another hormone—one that normally removes excess sugar. Insulin, produced by a group of cells within the pancreas,

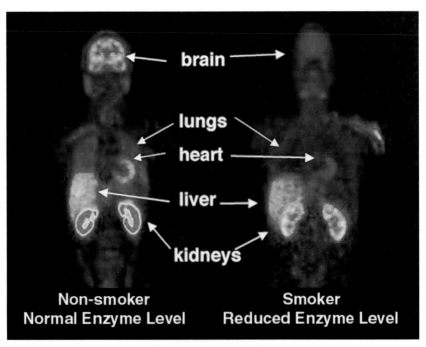

Research shows that smoking reduces the activity level of an enzyme called monoamine oxidase B (MAO-B), which plays an important role in breaking down chemicals in the body.

helps the body use sugar for energy. It also helps keep sugar in the blood at normal levels. But nicotine inhibits insulin, which results in the accumulation of an excess amount of glucose in the blood.

Changes to Brain

With the advancement of neuroimaging technologies, researchers have been able to learn more about what is going on in the brain when a person smokes tobacco. Through imaging studies, scientists have also gained a better understanding of brain function and how addiction affects certain regions of the brain, particularly the reward pathways. Because of the ability to "see" inside the brain, researchers have been able to document that changes in brain function are occurring as a result of smoking tobacco.

Chronic smokers have alterations in the biochemical and function of neurons in the brain occurs. These changes essentially damage the addicted person's brain circuits involved with emotion, motivation, and decision-making.

In 2006, researchers from the University of Bonn, in Germany, published the results of a brain imaging study that showed chronic smoking alters the chemical makeup of the brain. They collected detailed chemical data on brain metabolites taken from men and women participating in a smoking cessation program. The researchers compared their data with similar information obtained from healthy nonsmokers.

The results showed significant decreases in concentrations of a certain amino acid called N-acetylaspartate (NAA) in the part of the brain directly involved in the craving and relapsing behavior of addiction. Low amounts of NAA are also found in the brains of people with psychiatric and mood disorders, as well as alcohol and other substance abuse. When researchers followed up six months later, however, they found that the brain function of former smokers who had not relapsed had normalized. That is, they contained the normal levels of the amino acid.

Regular smokers are almost twice as likely as nonsmokers to have a particular allele identified by researchers.

Genetic Susceptibility to Addiction

Some research suggests that individual brain chemistry and genes play a major role in whether or not a person becomes addicted to nicotine. But just as blue eyes or brown hair are encoded in specific alleles, many aspects of the body's chemical response to nicotine is affected be the individual's genes.

Gene Variants and Dopamine

In the course of research on the role of dopamine in drug addiction, scientists have identified a number of alleles that appear to increase a person's risk for becoming addicted to nicotine. One allele has been found in habitual smokers almost twice as frequently as it occurs in people who do not smoke. A similar study also showed this allele was more common in heavy smokers than in light smokers.

Another study showed that a different allele appears more frequently in smokers and *pathological* gamblers— people who are addicted to gambling. Thus, scientists believe there may be a link between this allele and addictive behavior.

Nicotinic Cholinergic Receptors

Researchers have identified a large number of different types and configurations of nicotinic cholinergic receptors in the brain. The receptors consist of a combination up to five components, known as subunits.

A specific subunit of the receptor has been linked to nicotine addiction. In an experiment with mice that had been bred to lack the gene that produced this subunit, researchers observed that the mice with the missing gene did not experience the positive reinforcing properties of nicotine. In other words, they would not self-dose the drug. Apparently, the subunit plays a part in nicotine addiction.

Researchers have also discovered that certain nicotinic subunits have a greater sensitivity when exposed to nicotine than other subunits do. They release more dopamine and cause the user to have a more pleasurable reaction to the nicotine. Other subunits are far less sensitive to nicotine, which reduces the level of the pleasurable sensation that would normally occur with nicotine.

In animal studies, researchers have found that mice that are genetically coded to produce more sensitive nicotinic receptors are more likely to show signs of addiction to the chemical. Scientists suspect the same is true in humans, but further research is needed to determine if this is the case.

Peer pressure and role modeling at home are two of the social influences that can lead to smoking.

Nicotine Metabolism

Metabolism is the process by which substances in the body are broken down for energy or for other use. Studies have shown that when nicotine is broken down into inactive chemicals, the process occurs at different rates in different people.

In some people, a defect in the enzymes in the liver results in ineffective metabolism of nicotine. After smoking a cigarette, these people maintain higher levels of nicotine in the blood and brain than those without this genetic defect. Because of this gene, smokers do not need as many cigarettes as other people do. They smoke fewer cigarettes because they don't require more nicotine.

Investigators have also tried to learn more about the metabolism of nicotine itself. Nicotine exerts a powerful influence on the body through its effect on nicotinic receptors, but the body has mechanisms for clearing away toxic and harmful chemicals. This is one of the purposes of metabolism.

In the case of nicotine, most of this metabolism occurs in the liver, which is a storehouse of enzymes involved in breaking down and cleaning up harmful chemicals. Enzymes are chemicals that help the body per-

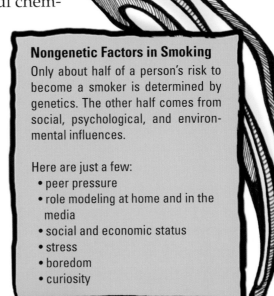

Nongenetic Factors in Smoking
Only about half of a person's risk to become a smoker is determined by genetics. The other half comes from social, psychological, and environmental influences.

Here are just a few:
- peer pressure
- role modeling at home and in the media
- social and economic status
- stress
- boredom
- curiosity

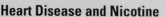

form necessary chemical reactions, such as breaking down sugars or building proteins.

In order to clear nicotine from the body, liver enzymes help change the nicotine into another chemical called cotinine. Unlike nicotine, cotinine does not bind to nicotinic receptors. For this reason, it does not have a powerful influence on the brain in the way nicotine does. Once nicotine is changed into cotinine, it can be more easily cleared from the body.

Heart Disease and Nicotine

When nicotine remains in the blood for a long time, it increases the amount of low-density lipoprotein (LDL) cholesterol, a wax-like substance that is normally found in all parts of the body. LDL is known as "bad" cholesterol because it leave deposits on the walls of blood vessels, causing them to eventually become clogged and hardened. High levels of LDL in the blood have been associated with in increased risk of coronary heart disease.

One of the enzymes on which scientists have focused their attention is known as CYP2A6. This enzyme is involved in metabolizing many chemical compounds, including nicotine. Just as with many other things in the body, the instructions for creating this enzyme are contained in a person's genetic makeup. In fact, genetic researchers have identified the multiple alleles that control the creation of CYP2A6.

The presence of two of these alleles seems to increase the probability that a person will be able to quit smoking. Among smokers, these alleles are also more common in light smokers than in heavy smokers. Some individuals have a resistance to nicotine addiction because they have an allele that decreases ability of the CYP2A6 enzyme to function. This slows the breakdown of nicotine. The presence of these specific alleles may help protect people from nicotine addiction. The research on these alleles may direct the development of medications that inhibit the function of the CYP2A6 enzyme in preventing and treating nicotine addiction.

Another enzyme, known as CYP2D6, also helps to convert nicotine to inactive cotinine. A number of recessive alleles have been shown to decrease the strength of the CYP2D6 enzyme, thus slowing the metabolism of nicotine. This slowing allows nicotine to stay active in the body for a longer period of time.

Internal View of the Heart

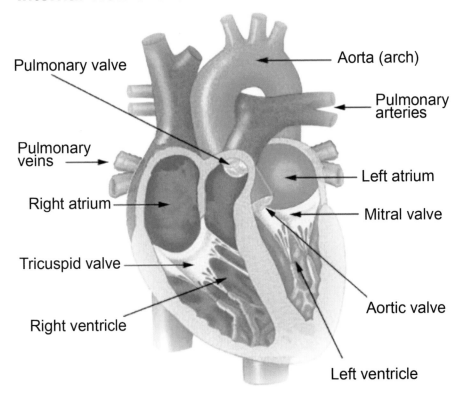

Nicotine increases the amount of LDL in the blood, which in turn increases the risk of coronary heart disease.

A number of other alleles seem to have the reverse effect, speeding up the metabolism of nicotine and clearing it from the body faster. Studies have shown that people with the alleles for rapid metabolism of nicotine are more likely to become heavy smokers. This may be because a person who clears his or her body of nicotine rapidly must smoke more cigarettes in order to maintain a high level of nicotine in his body. By smoking more often, a person is more likely to become addicted.

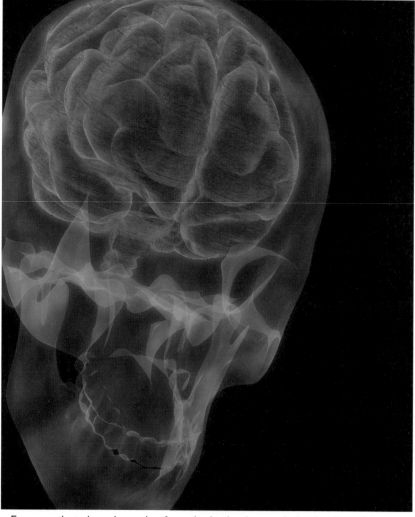

Enzymes that clear dopamine from the brain play a role in nicotine addiction.

Dopamine Metabolism

In addition to the liver enzymes that help clear nicotine from the body, other enzymes help regulate the work of neurotransmitters such as dopamine. Catechol-o-methyltransferase, COMT for short, is one of these enzymes. Another enzyme that helps clear dopamine from the brain is monoamine-oxidase, known as MAO.

When nicotinic receptors release dopamine, it floats around in the brain until it binds with a dopamine receptor. Although dopamine creates a feeling of euphoria and energy, excessive amounts of dopamine in the brain can be unhealthy. In the case of smoking, it is one factor that can lead to addiction. Enzymes like COMT and MAO clear dopamine from the brain, helping to ensure that the brain maintains a proper balance of neurotransmitters.

Numerous genes control the production of both COMT and MAO. Like the genes for the various receptors in the brain and body, genes controlling COMT and MAO have multiple possible allele combinations. Some of these combinations may put people at greater risk of becoming addicted to nicotine.

Certain alleles that may appear in the genes that control COMT and MAO can cause decreased or increased activity of these enzymes. Alleles that code for faster clearing of dopamine from the brain and alleles that cause increased nicotine metabolism have a similar effect on addiction. People who clear dopamine from their brains faster may be more likely to smoke more cigarettes in order to maintain higher levels

Risk of Relapse

While the painful symptoms of withdrawal are related to the effects of nicotine on the body, it is also influenced by behavioral and environmental factors. Certain experiences and memories can have a powerful effect on the brain and influence behavior and lead to relapse. For example, long after a smoker has quit, he or she may find that certain smoking cues such as the feel, smell, and sight of a cigarette produces intense cravings for nicotine.

of dopamine. This puts them at higher risk for addiction.

Using positron emission tomography (PET), a type of brain imaging, scientists have learned that unknown chemicals in tobacco smoke cause a decrease in the amounts of one form of the enzyme, known as MAO-A. This decrease in the enzyme causes an increase of dopamine levels that is unrelated to the increase caused by nicotine. These results show that nicotine is not the only chemical to alter the dopamine reward pathway. But more research is needed to determine what substances in tobacco smoke caused

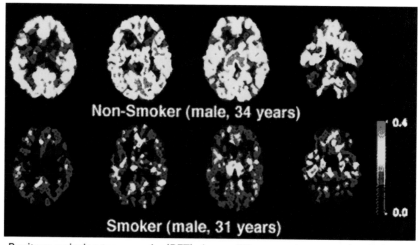

Positron emission tomography (PET) shows differences in enzyme levels in the brains of a smoker and a nonsmoker.

Behavioral and environmental factors can affect a person's chance of relapsing after quitting smoking.

this change. The increase of dopamine helps reinforce the smoker's likelihood of developing an addition.

Taste Perception

Taste is the sense by which the chemical qualities of foods or drugs placed in the mouth are distinguished by the brain. Chemical receptors in the nose, tongue, and processing centers in the brain all work together in response. These sensations are all sent to the brain, where they are analyzed and put together to come up with our individual perception of taste.

People do not share the same sense of taste. Some people will sense bitter or sour sensations that others do not. These varying abilities result from genetic varia-

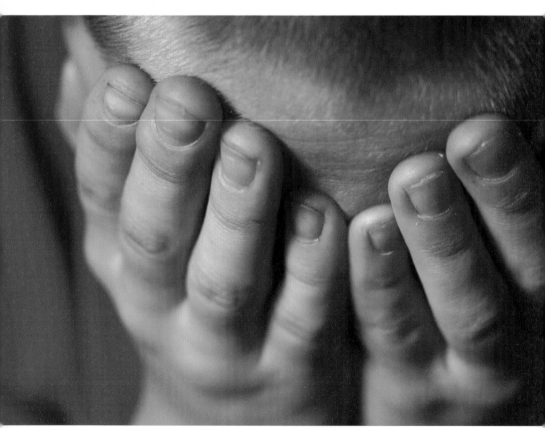

People suffering from depression are more likely to be smokers.

tions in a person's perception of taste, and can influence the sensations resulting from smoking. Genetic variants in taste perception could explain why some people respond negatively to the taste of tobacco and don't want to continue to use it, while others are not bothered. The person who finds the taste of cigarette smoke repulsive, however, is less likely to become a regular smoker. Some studies have shown that genetic influences on taste perception may influence addiction.

While a person's sense of taste may dissuade that individual from starting to smoke, he or she may still pick up the habit. Other behavioral or social pressures can influence the decision to start smoking.

Depression

A person's mental state can make a difference in whether a person smokes. Studies have shown that if a person is depressed, he or she may smoke more often. Other research has shown that people suffering from depression are more likely to be smokers than those who are not depressed. Whether the depression causes the smoking or the smoking is a cause of depression remains a question for debate. Regardless, there is a known association between the two conditions.

Depression is not simply a description of a person's mood. Someone who is sad is not necessarily depressed, even though many people use the word in that way. Clinical depression is a medical illness in which its symptoms last for more than two weeks. These symptoms include loss of interest in life, long-term feelings of sadness, and constant anger and bad moods.

How can the tendency for people suffering from depression to be smokers be explained through genetics? As it turns out, depression itself is also influenced by a person's genetic information. Many experts believe that one of the main causes of depression is an imbalance of neurotransmitters in the brain. A number of antidepressant medications are available to treat this imbalance, and many individuals have achieved good results when using these drugs to treat depression. On the other hand, these medications do not work for all people.

The Next Step

Scientists have made much progress in understanding the actions of neurotransmitters in the brain, nicotinic receptors, and genes involved in various aspects of addiction. Numerous studies point to how gene variants may play a role in whether or not a person develops

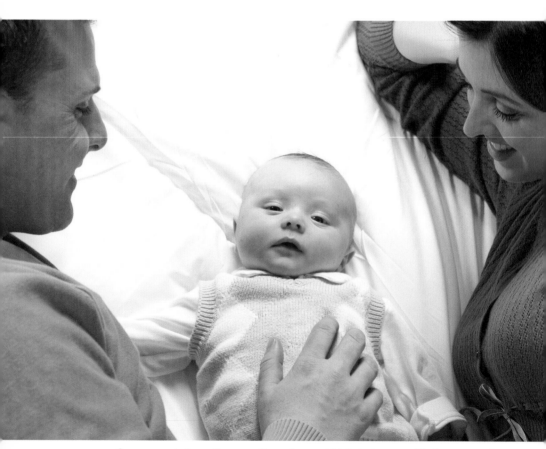

Some people have the genetic makeup at birth to be more likely to someday develop nicotine addiction.

While genetics does have an impact on how someone reacts to nicotine, learned behavior can also be a factor. If smoking is encouraged or a part of a person's culture, as was the case with this Filipino family, kids will be more likely to start smoking.

nicotine addiction. Genetic inheritance has shown some people may be more likely to become addicted to nicotine, while others are less likely.

Every person has a different brain chemistry, which itself is determined by a individual's genetic makeup. Gene variants can affect how a person will respond to smoking or whether he or she may be able to break nicotine addiction. Today, there are a number of methods available to help people quit smoking.

CHAPTER 6

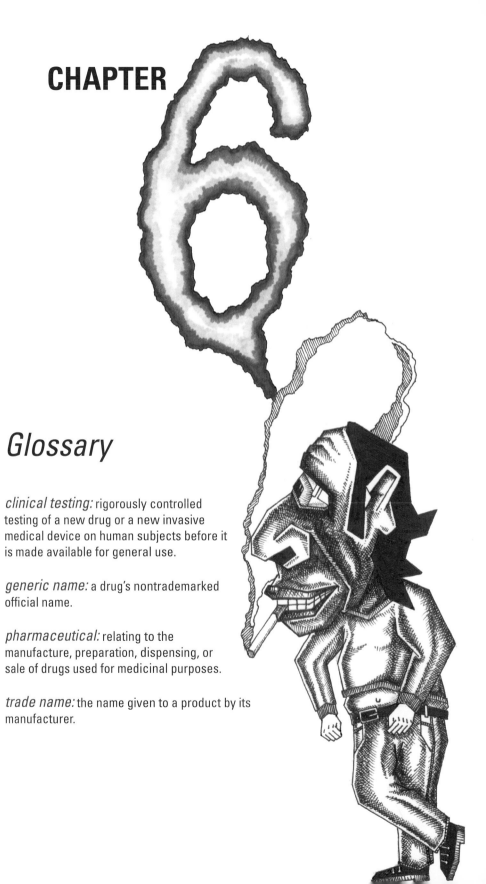

Glossary

clinical testing: rigorously controlled testing of a new drug or a new invasive medical device on human subjects before it is made available for general use.

generic name: a drug's nontrademarked official name.

pharmaceutical: relating to the manufacture, preparation, dispensing, or sale of drugs used for medicinal purposes.

trade name: the name given to a product by its manufacturer.

Overcoming Nicotine Addiction

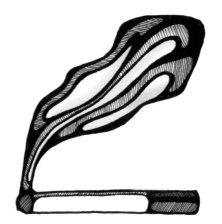

Julie smoked for almost a year before any of her friends found out about it. Most of them were a bit surprised, because she always went out of her way to eat healthy foods. They thought that someone as concerned with good health as she seemed to be would never put a cigarette to her lips.

One day Dale asked Julie about her smoking habit. "How did you ever get started smoking, Julie?" he asked. "I mean, you eat healthy stuff like tofu. I just don't get it."

"Well, I couldn't really help it, could I?" Julie replied, with a tinge of sarcasm in her voice. "My parents both smoked around me when I was a kid. They still do. I guess I was just destined to pick it up from them."

"Didn't I hear your dad's trying to quit?" Dale asked. "Maybe you could too."

"Actually, I tried once already," Julie said. "It didn't take. I hope my dad does better than me, but let's face it. It just isn't in my genes to quit smoking."

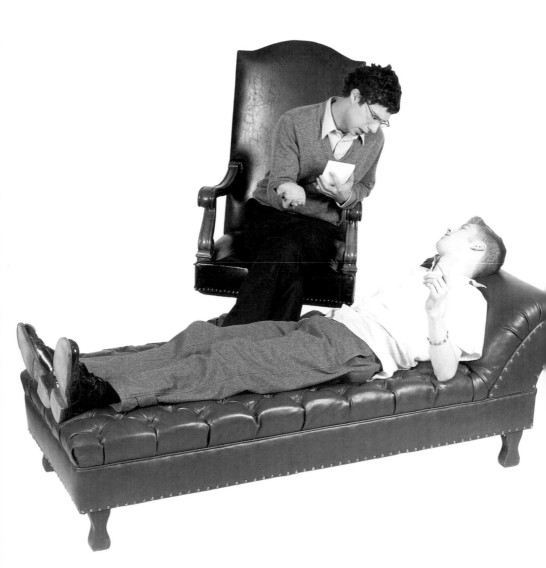

Talk therapy can provide smokers who are trying to quit with strategies for dealing with their intense cravings.

Quitting

Research on nicotine and genetics may one day help scientists develop a medication or vaccine to help people like Julie with her nicotine addiction. In the meantime, she has more options than smokers did twenty years ago.

Some of these treatments have drastically improved people's chances of breaking the smoking habit, although the medications aren't effective for everyone. Nevertheless, they do add important new weapons to the arsenal for people who are trying to quit using nicotine. The good news is that there are many options for people trying to quit today, and advancements in the study of genetics and nicotine is helping to make those options more effective.

Traditional Treatments

A common treatment for various kinds of addictions is a form of psychotherapy known as talk therapy. It is a behavioral treatment in which a patient works with a mental health counselor and sometimes with members of a group to express and try to resolve personal issues. Smokers who are trying to quit the habit attend talk therapy sessions in order to learn techniques to help them cope with nicotine cravings. These same methods are applied to help people deal with addictions to alcohol and other drugs.

For some people, the social aspect and support received from members of a talk therapy group leads to success. However, because nicotine holds its users so strongly in its control, talk therapies alone are not usually successful in helping people break the habit. In general, only 7 to 20 percent of people relying on these treatments alone can be expected to successfully quit.

Despite its low success rate, this form of treatment for addiction still plays an important role in helping people stop smoking. Talk therapies can help people understand the cues that cause them to have nicotine cravings, and show them ways to mentally fortify themselves against these cravings. Such strategies prove very useful to some people. For this reason, talk therapies are still widely used to help people quit smoking.

However, it is more common today to combine talk therapy with other kinds of options, including drug therapies. Studies have shown that a mixture of different treatment regimens, including both *pharmaceutical* and nonpharmaceutical options, is much more effective than talk therapy alone. In one study, almost 40 percent of people using a combination of talk therapy and nicotine patches were able to quit. That's far more than the average success rate for talk therapies alone.

Pharmaceutical Options

Today, there many pharmaceutical options that people can use to help them stop smoking. These drugs have been approved for use in treating nicotine addiction by the U.S. Food and Drug Administration—the government agency responsible for ensuring that drugs marketed in the United States are safe and effective. Smoking cessation aids include nicotine replacement therapy products, which are available by prescription or sold over-the-counter (OTC), and medications available only by prescription.

Nicotine Replacement Therapy (NRT)

The first widely used pharmaceutical aid to help people quit smoking, nicotine replacement therapy (NRT) seeks to help a person stop smoking by providing them with the very thing that smoking gives them—nicotine. While this method may seem somewhat self-defeating, the use of nicotine to help people stop quit smoking actually does work.

Basically, when a person craves a cigarette, what he or she really craves is nicotine. When a person tries to stop smoking, the amount of nicotine in his or her system begins to run low, and the body wants more. By using a form of NRT, the person receives a lower and safer dose of nicotine than he or she would have received by smoking or using another form of tobacco. NRT allows an individual to maintain a level of nicotine that satisfies

Some NRT products were initially prescription-only but later became available over the counter.

his or her cravings without having to rely on cigarettes to get it.

By controlling and gradually lowering the amount of drug that is delivered (NRT products come in varying doses), the nicotine user can slowly decrease the amount of drug the body craves. By allowing the body to adjust to decreasing levels of nicotine, a person can also avoid or reduce symptoms of withdrawal. Essentially, NRT treats a person's physical dependence on nicotine—reducing withdrawal symptoms and preventing

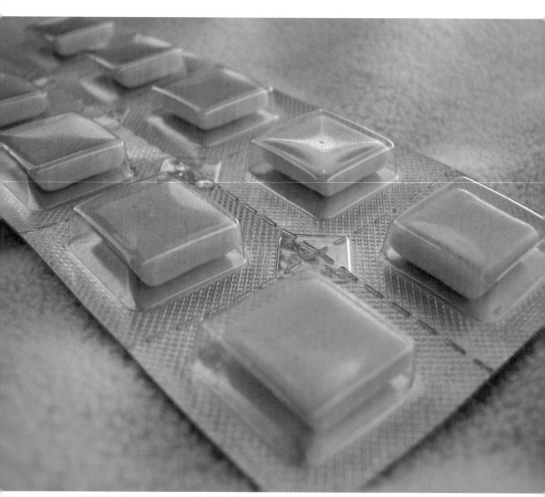

Nicotine gum was the first form of nicotine replacement therapy made available in the United States.

relapse, and allowing the person to concentrate on the behavioral and psychological treatments of addiction.

The first form of NRT to be made available in the United States was nicotine gum, which in 1984 was approved by the FDA as a pharmacological aid on a prescription-basis only for smoking cessation. This product allows people to give themselves nicotine whenever they feel a craving. Although nicotine delivered by chewing gum takes longer to reach the brain than it does when inhaled in cigarette smoke, the effects are still the same. Because of its effectiveness in helping nicotine users quit, nicotine gum was moved from prescription-only to general over-the-counter sale.

Another NRT product is the nicotine transdermal patch, a self-adhesive patch that delivers a relatively constant amount of nicotine through the skin to the person wearing it. It is available in dosage forms ranging from 5 mg/day to 21 mg/day. Using gradually decreasing dosage forms, an individual can reduce the level of nicotine in his or her system until being successfully weaned off the drug. Like nicotine gum, the transdermal patch was sold as a prescription drug when first approved by the FDA in 1991. The product also became available in 1996 as an OTC drug.

Other forms of NRTs include inhalers, nasal sprays, and lozenges. All are available for sale over the counter and, like the nicotine gum and transdermal patch, are meant to be used for a short period of time, typically a period of one to three months.

For the most part, all NRTs have had similar success in helping nicotine users break their addiction. On average, successful quitting rates are about 25 percent, as opposed to 5 to 10 percent without the drug. NRT is often used in combination with other therapies.

Zyban®/Wellbutrin® (Bupropion)

The first nicotine-free drug used for treating nicotine addiction is the antidepressant bupropion, which is also known by its *trade name* of Zyban. Available only by prescription, bupropion was approved by the FDA in 1997 for use in helping smokers quit. Patients take the drug for up to twelve weeks.

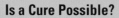

Is a Cure Possible?

Today, there is no medicine that can "cure" addiction. Medications such as Chantix and Zyban, as well as NRT products, can help people fight nicotine addiction, but they cannot stop a person from becoming addicted. Some researchers believe a better understanding of genetics and chemistry will make a cure possible one day, though they admit it may occur many years in the future. Others think the brain is too complicated and that a cure for addiction would require changing the chemistry of the brain in such a dramatic way that other systems in the body would be thrown out of balance.

The drug apparently works in the brain by slowing down the clearance of dopamine by the enzymes COMT and MAO. Because the amount of dopamine remains at elevated levels in the brain for a longer period of time, the person trying to quit smoking has fewer nicotine cravings. As a result, Zyban helps reduce the desire to smoke. The goal is to make the cravings gradually decline until the smoker no longer feels the need to have a cigarette at all.

Bupropion also appears to have an effect on nicotinic receptors. Some research indicates that the drug actually blocks nicotine from the nicotinic receptors. This reduces the effects of nicotine in the brain.

The effectiveness of bupropion varies. Doctors report that some patients have very positive responses to bupropion, while the drug simply doesn't seem to work for other people. Because they know the drug has the potential to work, most medical professionals continue to prescribe bupropion for nicotine addiction, as well as for depression.

Varenicline

Approved by the FDA in 2006, varenicline is the *generic name* for a medication intended for adults who want to quit smoking. Manufactured by the drug company

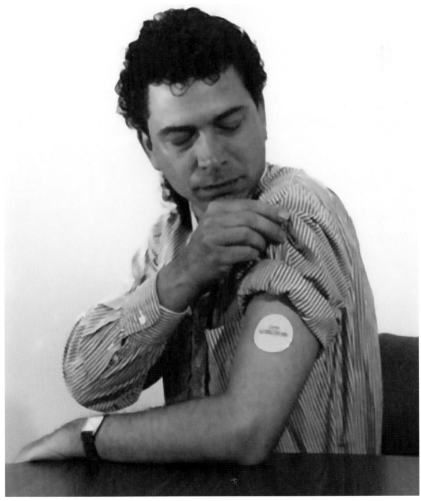

Nicotine transdermal patches wean smokers off nicotine with gradually decreasing dosages of the drug.

Drugs that regulate the level of dopamine in the brain can help decrease
nicotine cravings and withdrawal symptoms.

Pfizer under the brand name Chantix, varenicline works in a similar way that bupropion does—by releasing low levels of dopamine in the brain. This results in a decrease in nicotine cravings and withdrawal symptoms such as irritability, insomnia, and difficulty concentrating.

The History of Bupropion

In 1997, drug maker GlaxoSmithKline introduced a new drug to the market that was approved for use in the treatment of nicotine addiction. Actually, Zyban was simply a new name for an antidepressant the pharmaceutical company (then known as Glaxo Wellcome) first released in 1985 under the name Wellbutrin. Today, Zyban is often a physician's first choice in treating nicotine addiction.

Chantix nicotine molecules have a similar shape. As a result, Chantix molecules c will bind to nicotinic receptors in the same way that nicotine molecules do. When Chantix molecules bind to nicotinic receptors, they accomplish two things. First, they block nicotine molecules from reaching their target receptors. Since fewer nicotine molecules can bind to the receptors, the sensation of pleasure from smoking is reduced and, therefore, less addictive. Second, Chantix molecules stimulate the nicotinic receptors to release dopamine, although in smaller quantities than would occur with stimulation by nicotine molecules. The release of dopamine in small amounts helps relieve some of the smoker's withdrawal symptoms.

The approved course of treatment using Chantix is twelve weeks, although that amount of time can be safely doubled. On the Pfizer Web site for medical professionals, it is reported that Chantix "may produce mild physical dependence which is not associated with addiction." This means people using Chantix may require the medication (be dependent on it) to avoid nicotine withdrawal, but will not have an uncontrollable desire to continue using it after they are no longer addicted to nicotine.

In *clinical testing* of the drug's effectiveness, Chantix did well. Short-term data showed that the medication was more effective than bupropion in helping people quit smoking. Among patients who followed a twelve-week course of treatment with Chantix, 44 percent were able to quit smoking, compared with 30 percent of Zyban patients. Long-term data showed that a year after treat-

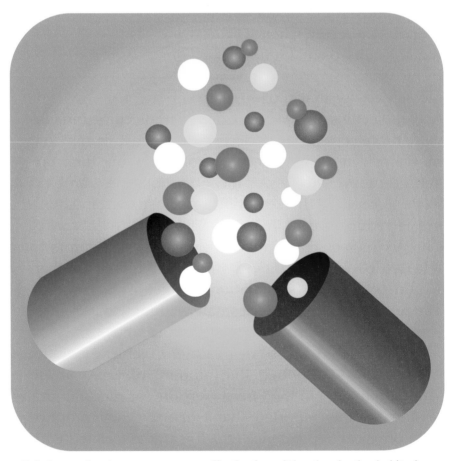

Talk therapy has been proven more effective for quitting the nicotine habit when combined with drug therapy.

ment with Chantix, 22 percent of participants had successfully quit smoking versus 16 percent of patients who had taken Zyban. Because the drug has been on the market for a relatively short amount of time, research on use of the medication is limited, however.

The FDA does not recommend that other smoking-cessation products be used along with Chantix. Its adverse effects include nausea, headache, and insomnia.

Black Box Warnings

In 2004, the Food and Drug Administration directed all pharmaceutical companies producing antidepressants to add black box warnings to the labels of those products. Black box warnings indicate the product carries the highest risk among all prescription medications. In the case of antidepressants, these warnings alert parents and others to the possibility of increased risk of suicidal thinking and behaviors in adolescents and children who are using these medications.

In early 2008, concerns about the drug's possible link to neuropsychiatric symptoms, such as changes in behavior, depression, or suicidal behavior, led Pfizer to add a black box warning to the drug's packaging and label.

Future Treatments

People trying to quit the nicotine habit today can turn for help to behavioral techniques such as talk therapy. These nonpharmaceutical treatments have proven more effective, however, when combined with pharmaceutical smoking cessation aids. However, the development of nicotine replacement therapy products, Zyban, and Chantix is just the beginning of a potentially large selection of pharmaceutical treatment options for people

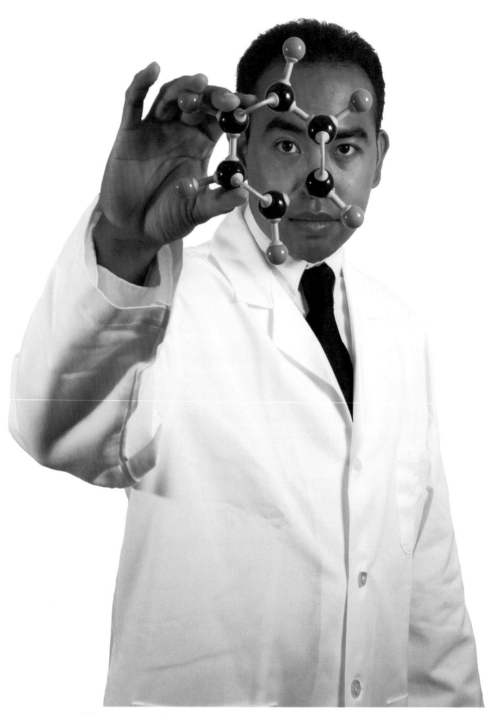

Pharmacogenetics seeks to understand why medications work well in some
people and not in others, depending on their genetic makeup.

interested in quitting smoking.

Pharmacogenetics

Patients often respond differently to the same drug. For example, a medication that is effective in one person may not work at all in another individual. And in some cases, a patient may suffer an adverse reaction from the drug. Drug researchers have found that much of this

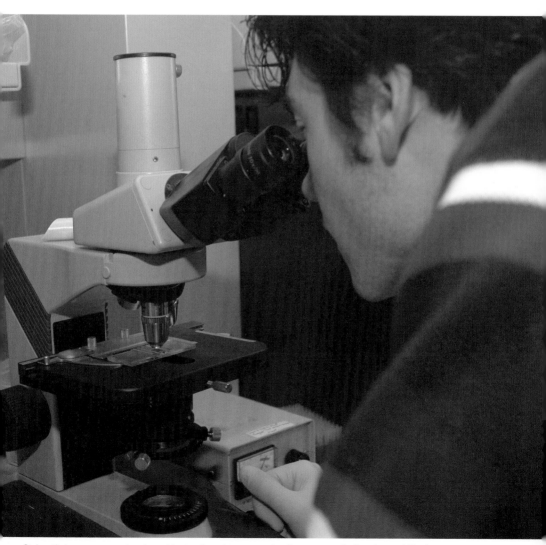

Scientists may one day be able to develop genetically targeted nicotine addiction treatments.

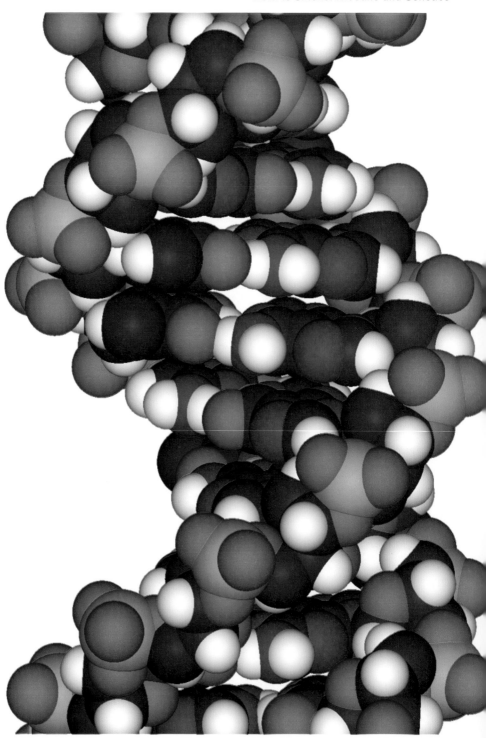

One important step in customizing drugs for individuals based on their genetics
is identifying the alleles involved in making people habitual smokers.

individuality in drug response is inherited, or genetically determined. The study of this variability in drug response is known as *pharmacogenetics*.

Pharmacogenetics combines pharmacological research with the latest advancements in genetic research. Scientists investigate the ways that certain drugs interact with people and evaluate their genetic makeup to try to determine why a medication works well in one person and doesn't in another. Pharmacogenetics seeks to understand why these differences occur and attempts to match people with the treatment options that will work best for them.

Research in pharmacogenetics may one day result in the creation of medications that are custom made for an individual's unique genetic information. Although the necessary scientific knowledge and technology to allow this is not available today, the understanding of individuality in drug response accomplished through pharmacogenetics research will contribute to the development of these potential medications.

Pharmacogenetics and Smoking Cessation

Pharmacogenetics holds a great deal of promise for the future of nicotine addiction treatment. But before scientists can develop genetically targeted nicotine addiction treatments, they must first identify the alleles involved in making people habitual smokers. And then researchers need to determine exactly how these alleles cause their influence. While it is important to identify these alleles in the research laboratory, it is even more important to be able to identify them in individuals seeking treatment to overcome nicotine addiction.

More information about the specific genes that influence the smoking habit and nicotine addiction is needed before physicians and counselors can turn to this tool for helping people with nicotine addictions. The current costs of genetic tests themselves are too expensive—they can range from hundreds to thousands of dollars.

However, when genetic testing does become more common in the family physician's office, the technology holds great potential. For instance, a man trying to quit smoking could meet with his family doctor and request help. The physician would be able to send the man to a genetics lab, where a battery of tests could be conducted to determine which, if any, alleles the man had that might contribute to his nicotine addiction.

Such tests could show that the patient had alleles that coded for rapid metabolism of nicotine. Then the man's

Genetic testing of the future might be able to show, for instance, that a patient has alleles that code for rapid metabolism of nicotine, leading to the most appropriate treatment for the patient.

doctor could write a prescription for a drug specifically designed to treat people with that trait. The patient might have been using bupropion, but not had much luck because bupropion does not address the metabolism of nicotine. Instead, it works to modify the clearance of dopamine.

On the other hand, genetic testing could help identify another man who has alleles that code for increased activity of COMT and MAO enzymes, which clear dopamine from the brain. This patient might benefit more from bupropion than he would from another drug.

This, then, is the promise of pharmacogenetics—the ability to match an individual to the drugs that will work best for that person. Current research has focused on identifying the exact genetic influences on smoking. In the future, as that goal is achieved, drug manufacturers may be able to turn their attention to making drugs that address specific genetic influences. Until then, smokers need to do the best they can with the treatment options that are currently available. Their lives depend on it.

Further Reading

Anderson, Judith. *Smoking (It's Your Health)*. North Mankato, Minn.: Smart Apple Media, 2005.

Balkin, Karen, and Helen Cothran (eds.). *Opposing Viewpoints Series: Tobacco and Smoking*. San Diego, Calif.: Greenhaven Press, 2004.

Connelly, Elizabeth Russell. *Nicotine = Busted!* Berkeley Heights, N.J.: Enslow, 2006.

Graham, Ian. Genetics: *The Study of Heredity (Investigating Science)*. Strongsville, Ohio: Gareth Stevens, 2002.

Hyde, Margret O., and John F. Setaro. *Smoking 101: An Overview for Teens*. Minneapolis, Minn.: Twenty-First Century Books, 2006.

Levert, Suzanne. *The Facts About Nicotine (Drugs)*. Tarrytown, N.Y.: Benchmark Books, 2006.

Stewart, Gail B. *Understanding Issues: Smoking*. San Diego, Calif.: KidHaven Press, 2002.

Stille, Darlene R. Genetics: *A Living Blueprint (Exploring Science: Life Science)*. Minneapolis, Minn: Compass Point Books, 2006.

For More Information

Basic Principles of Genetics: Mendel's Genetics
anthro.palomar.edu/mendel/mendel_1.htm

Facts About Smoking
rex.nci.nih.gov/NCI_Pub_Interface/Smoking_Facts/
about.html

How Stuff Works: Nicotine
 HYPERLINK "http://www.howstuffworks.com/
nicotine.htm" www.howstuffworks.com/nicotine.htm

KidsHealth: Smoking Stinks
www.kidshealth.org/kid/watch/house/smoking.html

KidsHealth: What is a Gene?
www.kidshealth.org/kid/talk/qa/what_is_gene.html

National Institute on Drug Abuse: NIDA for Teens:
The Science Behind Drug Abuse
teens.drugabuse.gov/facts/facts_nicotine1.asp

PBS: It's My Life: Smoking
pbskids.org/itsmylife/body/smoking

Surgeon General's Warning
www.gdcada.org/statistics/tobacco/surgeon/general.htm

Time: Addiction and the Brain
www.time.com/time/2007/addiction/

Publisher's note:
The Web sites listed on this page were active at the time of publication. The publisher is not responsible for Web sites that have changed their addresses or discontinued operation since the date of publication. The publisher will review and update the Web site list upon each reprint.

Bibliography

Batra, Vikas, Ashwin A. Patkar, Wade H. Berrettini, Stephen P. Weinstein, and Frank T. Leone. "The Genetic Determinants of Smoking." *Chest* 123 (2003): 1730–1739.

Berrettini, Wade H., E. Paul Wileyto, Leonard Epstein, Stephanie Restine, Larry Hawk, Peter Shields, Ray Niaura, and Caryn Lerman. "Catechol-O-Methyltransferase (COMT) Gene Variants Predict Response to Bupropion Therapy for Tobacco Dependence." *Biological Psychiatry* 61 (2007): 111–118.

Centers for Disease Control and Prevention, National Center for Health Statistics. *National Health Interview Survey*, 1965–2005, 2006.

Hunter, David. *Antidepressants and Advertising: Marketing Happiness*. Broomall, Pa.: Mason Crest, 2007.

Lemonick, Michael D. "How We Get Addicted." *Time*, July 5, 2007. http://www.time.com/time/magazine/article/0,9171,1640436,00.html.

Lerman, Caryn, Freda Patterson, and Wade Berrettini. "Treating Dependence: State of the Science and New Directions." *Journal of Clinical Oncology* 23(2) (2005): 311–323.

Lerman, Caryn, and Wade Berrettini. "Elucidating the Role of Genetic Factors in Smoking Behavior and Nicotine Dependence." American Journal of Medical Genetics Part B (Neuropsychiatric Genetics) 118B (2003): 48–54.

Martini, Frederic. Fundamentals of Anatomy and Physiology. 7th ed. San Francisco, Calif.: Benjamin Cummings, 2005.

Mineur, Yann S., and Marina R. Picciotto. "Genetics of Nicotine Acetylcholine Receptors: Relevance to Nicotine Addiction." Biochemical Pharmacology (June 2007).

Munafo, Marcus R., Alexandra E. Shields, Wade H. Berrettini, Freda Patterson, and Caryn Lerman. "Pharmacogenetics and Nicotine Addiction Treatment." *Pharmacogenomics* 6(3) (2005): 211–223.

Pfizer, Inc. "Pfizer for Professionals: Chantix." http://www.pfizerpro.com/brands/chantix.jsp.

Porth, Carol Mattson. *Pathophysiology: Concepts of Altered Health States*. 7th ed. Philadelphia, Pa.: Lippincott Williams & Wilkins, 2005.

United States Food and Drug Administration. "FDA Approves Novel Medication for Smoking Cessation," May 11, 2006. http://www.fda.gov/bbs/topics/NEWS/2006/NEW01370.html.

Index

addiction 17–19, 21, 23–25, 27, 29, 31, 59–61, 63–65, 67, 69, 71–72, 74–78, 81–83, 85, 87–89, 91–93, 95–97, 99, 101–102
alleles 38–45, 49, 55, 60–61, 71, 74–77, 101–103
animal studies 59–62, 72

bupropion 92–93, 95–96, 102–103

cancer 11, 13, 15–16, 36, 59
    lung 13, 59
    mouth 17
carcinogen 11, 13, 59
catechol-o-methyltransferase (COMT) 77, 92, 103
Centers for Disease Control (CDC)
Chantix 92, 95–97
clinical testing 84, 96
chromosomes 35, 37–38, 40, 42, 45, 47
Cotinine 74–75

dependence 19, 24, 64, 90, 96
depression 31, 80–82, 93,97
dopamine 20, 24–25, 27–29, 59, 67, 71–72, 76–78, 80, 92, 94–95,103
DNA 32, 34–40, 44–47, 49

enzymes 73–74, 76–77, 92, 103

genetics 14, 16, 18–19, 24, 28, 30, 33, 35–37, 39–49, 52, 54, 56, 58, 60, 663, 68, 70, 72, 74, 76, 78, 80–82, 86–88, 90, 92, 94, 96, 100, 102
genetic susceptibility 50, 59, 65, 71
genetic predisposition 50, 53, 63

genes 18–19, 33, 35, 37–39, 42, 45, 47–49, 52, 58–60, 64–65, 71, 77, 82, 86, 101
gene variants 71, 82–83
genome 32, 35, 38, 46, 52, 55, 58
genotype 50, 55–56

heart disease 11, 13, 53, 55, 74–75
heredity 11, 13, 32, 38, 53, 55, 74–75
hormones 28, 66–68
Human Genome Project 35, 46

metabolism 66, 73, 75–77, 102–103
Mendel, Gregor
monoamine oxidase (MAO) 68, 77–78, 92, 103

N-acetylaspartate (Naa) 69–70
National Cancer Institute 15
neurotransmitters 20, 24–26, 28–29, 77, 82
nicotine
    addiction to 17, 19, 21, 23, 25, 60–61, 63–65, 67, 71, 74–76, 82–83, 85, 87–89, 92–93, 95, 99, 101–102
    use of 19, 29, 59, 65, 90–91
nicotine replacement therapy (NRT) 88–92, 97
nitrogen bases 32, 35–36
nucleotides 35–36
nucleus accumbens 24–25, 27–28

pathology 66, 71
peer pressure 17, 72–73
Pfizer 95, 97
phenotype 50, 55–56
pharmacogenetics 98–99, 101, 103
population studies 60–63
proteins 37–38, 45, 47, 50, 52, 74

receptors 20, 25, 27–29, 71–74, 77, 80, 82, 92, 95
relapse 70, 78, 91
reward pathways 22–23, 27, 59, 67, 69, 78

sickle cell anemia 58
smokeless tobacco 16–17
smoking 11–17, 19, 21–23, 29, 52, 63–65, 67–69, 72–74, 76–79, 81, 83, 85–89, 91–92, 95–97, 99, 101, 103
smoking cessation (quitting) 69, 79, 88, 91, 97, 99, 101
stroke 13, 15

taste 59, 80–81
therapy
    drug 96
    talk 86–88, 96–97
tobacco 11, 13–17, 19, 27, 29, 31, 59, 64, 69, 78, 81, 89
tolerance 20, 24, 29
trait 19, 39–42, 44–45, 47, 49, 52, 55, 57–58, 63, 102
twin studies 63

United States Food and Drug Administration (FDA) 88, 91–93, 97

Varenicline 93, 95
ventral tegmental area (VTA) 23–25, 27

Wellbutrin 95
withdrawal 20, 24, 29–31, 78, 90–91, 94–96

Zyban 92, 95, 97

Picture Credits

Centers of Disease Control and Prevention: p. 12

Dreamstime.com
  Caraman, p.64
  Laurenthamels: p. 82
  Moori: p. 90

istockphoto.com
  ChristianAnthony: p. 76
  Dra_schwartz: p. 89
  Gil, Jose: p. 98
  Geopaul: p. 26, 30, 96
  Spectral-Design: p. 34
  Thompson, Leah-Anne p. 94

Jupiter Images: p. 18, 70, 71, 80, 82, 86

National Cancer Institute: pp. 17, 57
  Branson, Bill, p. 53
  Bartlett, Linda, p.61, 62

National Human Genome Research Institute (NHGRI): pp. 48, 49, 54
  Bartlett, Maggie: p. 58
  Leja, Darryl, pp. 46, 47,

Surveillance Epidemiology and End Results (SEER), a program of the National Cancer Institute (NCI): p. 75

To the best knowledge of the publisher, all other images are in the public domain. If any image has been inadvertently uncredited, please notify Harding House Publishing Service, Vestal, New York 13850, so that rectification can be made for future printings.

Author/Consultant Biographies

Author

David Hunter is the author of a number of books targeted toward young people and focused on issues of health and wellness. He served in the Peace Corps as a junior high-level teacher in the Central Pacific island country of Kiribati. He is currently studying nursing at Johns Hopkins University and working as a clinical nurse extern at Johns Hopkins Hospital.

Consultant

Wade Berrettini, the consultant for *Smoking: The Dangerous Addiction*, received his MD from Jefferson Medical College and a PhD in Pharmacology from Thomas Jefferson University. For ten years, Dr. Berrettini served as a Fellow at the National Institutes of Health in Bethesda, Maryland, where he studied the genetics of behavioral disorders. Currently Dr. Berrettini is the Karl E. Rickels Professor of Psychiatry and Director, Center for Neurobiology and Behavior at the University of Pennsylvania in Philadelphia. He is also an attending physician at the Hospital of the University of Pennsylvania.

Dr. Berrettini is the author or co-author of more than 250 scientific articles as well as several books. He has conducted ground-breaking genetic research in nicotine addiction. He is the holder of two patents and the recipient of several awards, including recognition by Best Doctors in America 2003–2004, 2005–2006, and 2007–2008.